I0220645

Edward Webster Bemis, John Haynes

Local Government in the South and the Southwest

Edward Webster Bemis, John Haynes

Local Government in the South and the Southwest

ISBN/EAN: 9783337005061

Printed in Europe, USA, Canada, Australia, Japan

Cover: Foto ©ninafisch / pixelio.de

More available books at **www.hansebooks.com**

LOCAL GOVERNMENT

IN THE

SOUTH AND THE SOUTHWEST

POPULAR ELECTION

OF

UNITED STATES SENATORS

JOHNS HOPKINS UNIVERSITY STUDIES

IN

HISTORICAL AND POLITICAL SCIENCE

HERBERT B. ADAMS, Editor

History is past Politics and Politics present History.—*Freeman*

ELEVENTH SERIES

XI–XII

LOCAL GOVERNMENT IN THE SOUTH AND THE SOUTHWEST

BY PROF. EDWARD W. BEMIS, PH. D. (J. H. U.),

AND

Students in Vanderbilt University

POPULAR ELECTION OF U. S. SENATORS

BY JOHN HAYNES,

Graduate Student in Johns Hopkins University

BALTIMORE

THE JOHNS HOPKINS PRESS

PUBLISHED MONTHLY

November-December, 1893

COPYRIGHT, 1893, BY THE JOHNS HOPKINS PRESS.

THE FRIEDENWALD CO., PRINTERS,
BALTIMORE.

CONTENTS.

LOCAL GOVERNMENT IN THE SOUTH AND THE SOUTHWEST.

INTRODUCTION.

The following papers on local government in the South were undertaken by the writers when seniors or graduate students in my classes at Vanderbilt University, 1891-2. In all cases, save Missouri, it was possible for the investigator to take his own State or the State in which he had recently resided.

It is believed that the recent growth here shown of local government in Kentucky, Texas, Mississippi, Florida, South Carolina, Georgia, Missouri, and Arkansas, will appear significant of greater changes in the future. There is confirmation of my statement of ten years ago: "As the New England town was built up about the church, so the Western and Southern town is centering its political activity about the school."[1]

Wherever there is in any Southern State any consideration at all by the voters of local taxes for any local purpose, the purpose is almost sure to be the improvement of the public school. The rapid growth of the public school system in the South will certainly strengthen this beginning of local government. Then we must observe the great number of small incorporated towns or villages in this section, where as few as 500 inhabitants in a hamlet often secure considerable rights of government in a municipal organization.

It will be of great interest to the general reader or the student of political science to note the proof in North Caro-

[1] Johns Hopkins University Studies in Historical and Political Science, Vol. I., No. 5.

lina that it is impossible to force upon a State institutions of a higher type than the intelligence, habits and prejudices of the average voter have prepared him to use. The failure of the town-meeting in North Carolina when introduced by a carpet-bag government teaches a valuable lesson. Even in that State, however, especially in its western part, where the percentage of whites, and probably of intelligence, is higher than in the eastern part, there is, as I have discovered in traveling through it, a growing desire for a gradual abandonment of what is now the most complete system of State control and centralization of local government in this country.

Whatever may have been the influence of early geographical, religious and social conditions in diverting the South from a development of local government such as Jefferson praised in New England and wanted in the South, I am convinced that its rapid growth now is prevented only by the presence of a large colored population that is considered as yet incapable of making wise use of democratic institutions.

In Kentucky in 1890 there were only 14.4 colored to every 85.6 white, and not a county in which the colored were in the majority. In Missouri there were only 5.7 colored persons to 94.3 white. In Tennessee there were 24.4 colored to 75.6 white, and three counties had more colored than white. In Arkansas there were 27.4 colored to 72.6 white, and in the fourteen counties possessing a majority of colored out of seventy-eight counties of the State there were 72,104 white to 154,618 colored.

Texas, thanks in part to a systematic and determined effort in some portions of the State to keep out all colored people, had only 21.9 colored to 78.1 white, and in only fifteen counties out of two hundred and forty do the colored predominate, with 126,368 to 82,310 whites. In twenty-nine counties, with 8,848 whites, no colored are reported in the census. In eleven others, with 5,291 whites, there is only one colored person to a county. In one of these, as a resident informs me, there are numerous signboards with the inscription, " Mr. Darkey, don't let sundown find you in this county!" In twenty-seven other counties of Texas there are 66,487 whites and only 2,462 colored. In no one of these counties are there more than ten colored, while there are thirty-nine other counties in no one of which are there one hundred colored, but only an average of thirty-eight, while there are 149,702 whites, or an average of 1,465. Finally, in the forty-four remaining counties of Texas there are 572,684 whites to only 44,061 colored, a ratio of thirteen to one.

In North Carolina there are 62.2 whites to 34.8 colored, and fifteen of the ninety-six counties have a majority of colored, the figures being 116,599 white to 170,113 colored.

The western half of North Carolina, the eastern half of Kentucky, the eastern third of Tennessee, three-fourths of Texas, and nearly all of Missouri are undisturbed by the race question. As a result local government is advancing steadily in Missouri, Kentucky, and Texas, and seems to be kept back in North Carolina, and possibly Tennessee, by the different race conditions in the larger part of those States. The situation has been more difficult in the other Southern States.

In Florida there are only 57.5 whites to every 42.5 colored, and ten of the forty-five counties, embracing 43.8 per cent. of the entire population of the State, have 62,310 whites to 104,654 colored. In Alabama, where there are 55.1 whites to 44.1 colored, there are twenty counties of the sixty-six in the State which have 157,655 whites to 406,087 colored; and in Georgia, with 46.7 per cent. colored, there are thirty-five of the eighty-four counties that have 199,006 white to 235,339 colored. In making these latter computations, beginning with Florida, no county in any State is included where a majority is not colored.

In Louisiana 50.1 per cent. were colored. In thirty-three of the fifty-nine parishes, corresponding to the counties of other States, there were in 1890 only 174,349 whites to 376,-668 colored; while in Mississippi, with 57.6 per cent. colored, forty of the seventy-five counties had 258,096 whites to 606,-310 colored. These forty counties embrace sixty-seven per cent., or two-thirds of the population of the State.

In South Carolina 60.7 per cent. were colored. In twenty-seven of the thirty-five counties the colored exceeded the whites, and in each of thirteen counties the colored were more than twice as numerous as the whites.

Democratic institutions cannot be based upon an ignorant suffrage, as the fifteenth amendment vainly attempted. An unwritten chapter of American history will some time reveal the effort of the late President Hayes and a majority of the dominant party in Congress, shortly after the war, to prevent the passage of the fifteenth amendment. Instead, there was desired a limitation of the suffrage among the blacks to those who could pass some educational test. Such a result of the war had been anticipated without ill-feeling by General Wade Hampton in his parting addresses to his soldiers, and would have been satisfactory to most of his fellow-officers of the Confederacy. Mr. Hayes, then just elected from Ohio to the lower house, secured the adoption of his views by nearly all the caucuses of the Republican Congressmen held by States. Then, if his account to the writer, in August, 1892, of his struggle was not wholly mistaken, he was forced to witness a complete overpowering of his wishes and those of the majority by the impetuous eloquence and bitter partisanship of the older party leaders in the general congressional caucus that followed. Nowhere, as he put it, is a newly-elected member so unable, even when he is in a small majority, to successfully oppose older leadership, as in Congress. It seems that all the facts on this grave matter do not appear in Blaine's *Twenty Years in Congress.* Out of the defeat of that liberal policy of Mr. Hayes have come sad results in all phases of Southern life; but with the gradual education of the Southern youth in the rapidly rising schools, and the recent tendency to restrict the suffrage by direct or indirect educational tests, a growth of local government becomes more and more attractive to the Southern educators and leaders of public opinion. The result will be somewhat evident in the following pages, but much more so as time goes on.

Some who have written short chapters in this monograph have not been able to investigate as fully as others; though it has not been the object to write in such detail upon any State as was done in the earlier volumes of the Studies, when it was deemed wise to devote an entire monograph to a single State. Only salient features have here been touched upon. The papers are printed almost verbatim as written by their authors, except as omission of details has been found necessary. Unfortunately the students who were to take Mississippi and Louisiana were forced to abandon the work when too late for substitutes to be found, while no one was secured for Florida; but the editor has written one or two brief paragraphs on each of these three States, merely to prevent their entire omission and to give a few such characteristics as appear in their latest legislation. South Carolina and Virginia have been already treated in the Studies (South Carolina in Vol. I., No. 12, 1883, and Virginia in Vol. III., Nos. 2-3). But the interesting growth of local government in South Carolina since the appearance of Volume I. of the above Studies in 1883 has been briefly described.

North Carolina, Tennessee, Louisiana, Alabama, Georgia, and Mississippi are first treated and in the above order, which roughly represents the present development of the power of local taxation, North Carolina having the least. None as yet possesses the power of local taxation save in incorporated towns, cities and special school districts. Then follow South Carolina, Florida, Texas, Arkansas, Kentucky, and Missouri, in all of which all the school districts, and in the last two all of the townships, have powers of local taxation whose exercise is steadily increasing.

This series of papers is published in the hope that the accounts here given of the development in so many Southern States, since 1880, of such local institutions as have long prevailed in the North and West, will serve to further knit together all sections of our common country, and will stimulate the friends of local government in the South to persevere in a work already so well begun and so well calculated to secure better schools and better political institutions of every kind.

EDWARD W. BEMIS.

UNIVERSITY OF CHICAGO,
September. 1893.

I

LOCAL GOVERNMENT IN NORTH CAROLINA.

The old buccaneers are said to have buried, on the long, low sandy beaches of Carolina's coast, rich booty from many a gallant ship. On stormy nights, when the winds howl and the waves roll high, the dim outline of the treasure-hunter may be seen against the darkling clouds, as he searches for the hidden gold. But the sea and the moon are loyal to the buccaneers, and the treasure-hunter toils in vain. But while Carolina refuses to give up her mythical treasures of Spanish gold, there are hidden treasures within her bounds that are only awaiting the search-light of history to reveal their beauty and their worth. To the student of history she opens an inviting field.

Perhaps no one trait of the early settlers of America was more prominent than their adaptability to their surroundings. In New England, the first inhabitants settled in tiny communities around their favorite ministers, and were closely bound together by the ties of church and by the necessity of presenting a united front to their enemies, the Indians. Quite naturally the town became the unit of government, and the town-meeting became the center around which was developed that spirit of independence and love of self-government which has ever characterized the New Englanders. In the South, however, especially in Virginia and the Carolinas, the early inhabitants came not so much for religious reasons as on account of a roving disposition and a desire of adventure and fortune. Instead of settling close together, they built their homes upon large plantations, oftentimes many miles apart, and connected only by the intricate channels of the streams that intersect this portion of the coast. These large estates, tilled by indentured white persons and by negro slaves, resembled in a

measure the manorial estates in England after the Norman
Conquest, and we shall find that in the development of local
self-government these lords followed very largely in the foot-
steps of their generation in England, and did not go back to
the town-meeting of their older ancestry, as did the inhabi
tants of New England. These large estates were not con-
ducive to the development of mutual dependence. The mas-
ter of each estate, surrounded by his broad acres, his tenants
and his slaves, took scant time to think of, much less discuss,
the petty subjects that were interesting the town-meetings of
the North. As for himself, his opinions were convictions, and
he gave little thought to the political education of the poorer
classes of whites. Says Thomas Nelson Page: " He believed
in a democracy, but understood that the absence of a titled
aristocracy had to be supplied by a class more virtuous than
he believed them to be. This class was, of course, that to
which he belonged." Such a system was peculiarly adapted
to the development of leaders, and the history of the Revolution and the first half-century of our country will show " such
a group of consummate leaders as the world has seldom seen
equaled."

   In the charter granted by Charles II. to Edward, Earl of
Clarendon, and others, as true and absolute Lords Proprietors
of Carolina, provision was made for the division of the territory into counties, and for enacting laws and constitutions for
the people of that province by and with the consent of the
freemen or their delegates. While this charter contained the
germ of representative government, it also contained an egg
that was soon to hatch out a brood of constitutional farces
such as the world had never before seen. Under that provision of the charter which granted the Lords Proprietors the
right of making " laws and constitutions," the Earl of Shaftesbury, the learned but visionary statesman, and John Locke,
the profound philosopher, drew up that stupendous travesty
on constitutional government, " The Fundamental Constitutions of Carolina." On Carolina's soil was the only continued
attempt made to connect political power with hereditary

wealth and to introduce into the wilds of America the effete system of feudalism as it existed in the England of the seventeenth century. While many of its provisions might appeal to the traditions and sentiments of the past, many of them were not only distasteful but absolutely detrimental to every interest of free government, and could only have originated in the brain of a visionary statesman or of a philosopher who had failed to bring his philosophy home to men's business and bosoms. Neither of these men had grasped that fundamental principle of government that political institutions must be growths. They cannot spring, Minerva-like, full-armed from Jove's brain. Their development must be gradual and their growth steady.

Under "The Fundamental Constitutions" the government of the province was vested in the hands of the eight Lords Proprietors, which body became not only an hereditary corporation but also a close corporation. The whole province was divided into counties, each county to consist of eight signiories, eight baronies, and four precincts.[1] By this division of the province into counties the process of making a nation by uniting the shires was reversed. The county, however, resembled in some respects our modern circuit court district. The precinct was the real unit of division and corresponded more nearly to the county in England. In fact, by act of the General Assembly in 1738, the precincts were altered to counties.[2] Provision was made for a court in each precinct, presided over by a steward and four justices of the precinct. This court had jurisdiction over all criminal cases, except those punishable with death and those pertaining to the nobility, and over all civil cases whatsoever. From this precinct court appeal could be made to the county court, which consisted of one sheriff and four justices, one for each precinct. Besides these two courts, "in every signiory, barony, and manor, the respective lord shall have power, in his

---

[1] Fundamental Constitutions, §3.
[2] Laws of N. C., 1738, c. 21, s. 1.

own name, to hold leet-court there." Here we have the transition from the old English township with its "reeve," "beadle," and "tithing-man," to the "manor," with its lord's steward and bailiff; and as the manor had not entirely lost its self-government, so the "grand model" provided for a court-leet, an interesting though fragmentary survival of the town-meeting. In the county court and precinct court mentioned above we recognize the form of the old English county court or Court of Quarter Sessions, though the resemblance can be more readily traced later when the functions of both courts were united into one. And this "Court of Pleas and Quarter Sessions," as it was afterwards called, remained in force until the Civil War, a mighty bulwark of the people's liberties.

While a few of the provisions of the "grand model" might appeal to the traditions and sentiments of the past, the great majority of them were not only distasteful but absolutely detrimental to every interest of free government. "Two-fifths of the land was to be perpetually annexed, one-fifth to the proprietors, the other to the hereditary nobility, leaving the remaining three-fifths among the people." "There shall be just as many landgraves as there are counties, and twice as many caziques, and no more. These shall be the hereditary nobility of the province, and by right of their dignity be members of parliament." "In every signiory, barony, and manor, all the leet-men shall be under the jurisdiction of the respective lords of the said signiory, barony, or manor, without appeal from him. Nor shall any leet-man or leet-woman have liberty to go off from the land of their particular lord and live anywhere else, without license obtained from their said lord, under hand and seal." "All the children of leet-men shall be leet-men, and so to all generations." In consequence of provisions like these we are not surprised to learn that this "grand model" was never put into practical operation and that it finally died a natural death. Thus the first

---

[1] Fundamental Constitutions, §16.   [2] Ibid., §4.   [3] Ibid., §9.
[4] Ibid., §22.   [5] Ibid., §23.

attempt to force ready-made institutions upon Carolina soil
failed, presaging the fate of a similar attempt in her later
history.

As we have intimated above, the first constitution contained the germ of representative government, but, unfortunately, what the course of proprietary legislation for the
first fifty years after the settlement of the colony was, there
are no accessible means of ascertaining.[1] Consequently we
can judge of this period only by the development the institutions had attained in 1715, the date from which the records
have been preserved; resting assured, however, that those
sturdy planters along the Chowan were not slow to realize the
powers and possibilities that lay in the court of Pleas and
Quarter Sessions. It became the unit of local government
in North Carolina and the center around which moved all
that pertained directly to the people in the administration of
government. Besides its administrative and civil duties it
performed the following functions, which, in Massachusetts,
would have been attended to by the people assembled in the
annual town-meeting, or by their officers elected in town-
meetings. It provided standard weights and measures, appointed constables,[2] and levied taxes for all county purposes.
It had the power of purchasing land and erecting houses
thereon for county purposes. It established and discontinued
ferries, roads, and bridges, and had complete supervision over
them, regulating tolls of ferries, appointing overseers of the
roads, and erecting bridges at the expense of the county.
While in some respects this county court government may
not compare favorably with the township government of the
North, still we must not judge it too harshly. While the
people of North Carolina did not have the privilege of meeting together annually and, in town-meeting assembled, of leg-

---

[1] Laws of N. C., 1821, vol. I., preface v.

[2] After 1833 the constables were elected in each Captain's district.
a military division of the county that must contain a population of
thirty-six men liable to perform military duty. Laws of N. C., 1831,
c. VIII.

islating upon all the minor points of interest in their several
districts, still they had their familiar court days, on which it
was a rare occasion when every community in the county was
not represented. Here, under the kindly shade of the court-
yard trees, the yeomanry and the landed proprietors met on
common ground and discussed politics, the price of cotton or
perchance of turpentine, and various other questions of peren-
nial interest. This was the forum of the farmers, the thought
exchange of the people; and he would have been a poor justice of the peace who could not have found out the prevailing
sentiments of his fellow-citizens on local affairs, and a worse
one, knowing that sentiment, had he failed to act accordingly.
Again, the county court flourished before the days of the
cheap politician. Then a public office was a public trust, and
then politics itself was reckoned a noble profession. The
honor and integrity of the well-to-do farmers who, in most
cases, constituted the county court, were unimpeached and
unimpeachable. The system not only developed a self-
respect in the members of the court, but, what was of more
importance, it fostered and nurtured a spirit of confidence in
the administration of the government among all classes of the
people.

The silent shifting of authority from King to Congress
made but slight change in this institution. The disturbance
occasioned by the transition was hardly perceptible. By the
constitution of 1776 the Governor was vested with authority to
appoint the justices of the peace for the several counties, on
recommendation of the Representatives in the General Assembly.[1] Some new duties devolved upon them, and their
powers were somewhat increased from time to time. After
1777 the county court was empowered to elect annually a
trustee for the county, whose duty it should be to collect all
moneys due the county. However, a majority of the justices of the peace in any county might abolish the office of
trustee, in which case the sheriff should perform all duties of

---

[1] Constitution N. C., 1776. XXXIII.

that officer.   In 1846 the justices of the peace were authorized to elect wardens of the poor, who, heretofore, had been elected by the freeholders.   Another duty that devolved upon the county court was the appointing of a patrol committee of three, whenever such precaution was deemed necessary, in each Captain's district in the county.[1]

But what of public schools?   Unfortunately they play a nominal part in local affairs prior to the years immediately preceding the Civil War.   Although the constitution of 1777 had resolved that schools should be established by the Legislature, " for the convenient instruction of youth," very little progress was made for many years.   It was not until 1844 that the counties were divided into school districts.   The voters of these several school districts elected annually a school committee of three, who had power to purchase land for school purposes, to build school-houses, and to administer the meager appropriations received from the State " Literary Fund."   This fund was distributed annually among the several counties of the State, and was supplemented by a tax levied by the court of Pleas and Quarter Sessions, which was not to be less than one-half of the estimated amount to be received by the county from the " Literary Fund."   However, "no county court shall tax any free person of color for the support and maintenance of common schools, and no person descended from negro ancestors to the fourth generation inclusive shall be taught in said schools."[2]

Such in brief is a sketch of local government in North Carolina prior to the Civil War.   Up to this time the growth and development of county government had progressed smoothly and quietly.   But the shock of civil strife left the internal organs of government in a fearfully deranged condi-

---

[1] Among other duties, the patrol was to visit the negro houses in their respective districts, as often as was deemed necessary, and to " inflict a punishment, not exceeding fifteen lashes, on all slaves they may find off their owner's plantations, without a proper permit or pass."   Revised Code N. C., 1855, c. 83, s. 3.

[2] Revised Code, 1855, c. 66, s. 33.

tion. With the proud prestige of statehood gone, with her hopes blighted and her prospects blackened, torn, mangled and bleeding, she lay an easy prey to the political vultures that swarmed upon her. Under the Reconstruction acts of Congress, a constitutional convention was called, and a constitution was framed and adopted in 1868. Again was the experiment tried of forcing a ready-made form of government on the people, and again was illustrated the principle that institutions must be growths. In this constitution, provision was made for the introduction of a system of local government resembling that which exists in Pennsylvania. Each county should elect biennially five commissioners. These commissioners had general supervision and control of the penal and charitable institutions, schools, roads, bridges, and levying of taxes, and were empowered to divide their respective counties into districts. In each of these townships there were, biennially, to be elected a clerk and two justices of the peace, who, under the supervision of the county commissioners, were to have control of the taxes, roads and bridges of the township. Furthermore, the township was empowered to elect a township school committee of three persons. Theoretically these changes were along the right lines. It divided the counties into townships and gave them a species of local government much superior in theory, at least, to anything they had before. It gave the masses of voters privileges which hitherto they had not enjoyed. Again, it was no new, untried scheme of government; it had been in successful operation in many of the Northern and Western States. Yet we shall not have to go far to find the reason that made it repugnant to a majority of that class of people who had ruled the State for a hundred years. Besides bearing the odium of being fathered by the hated carpet-bag government, it struck, as they thought, at the foundation of free government, when it placed the property-owners of the whole eastern section of the State at the mercy of the recently enfranchised slaves, by turning over to them the whole machinery of county government.

In 1875 the State government passed into the hands of the opposite political party, and the so-called "negro rule of the Reconstruction era" was over. Immediately a constitutional convention was called and a constitution was framed whose points of difference from the one it superseded were few but far-reaching. This constitution left the thirteen sections of Article VII., which pertained to municipal corporations, including county and township governments, intact, but added a fourteenth which gave the General Assembly "full power by statute to modify, change or abrogate any and all of the provisions of this section, and substitute others in their place, except sections seven, nine, and thirteen" (these sections limiting taxing and debt-making powers of municipal corporations).[1]

This section virtually threw the whole question of local government into the hands of the General Assembly elected soon after the ratification of the constitution. This legislature promptly availed itself of this section to do away with the existing local government by repealing all sections of Article VII. (save seven, nine, and thirteen). While the township itself was not destroyed, all its functions were taken from it. The right of electing the five commissioners and the school committee was taken away from the people. Under the new system the legislature appoints five justices of the peace in each township (but if there is an incorporated town in a township it has six justices, and one additional for every 1000 inhabitants) who hold office for six years. On the first Monday in June of every other year, they meet at the court-house and elect not more than five nor less than three commissioners. The board of county commissioners holds regular meetings on the first Monday in December and June. Upon their shoulders rest the internal affairs of the county; they look after the paupers of the county; they have supervision of jails, court-houses and other property of the county; they hear and determine all petitions for open-

---

[1] Constitution of 1876, Art. VII., s. 14.

ing or changing public roads; they build all bridges, provided said bridges do not cost over $500 each;[1] they establish polling places and appoint judges of election for each precinct; they make out the jury list, and they have complete supervision of the taxing machinery of the county. Annually the board of commissioners meets in session with the justices of the peace, and they perform such duties as devolve upon them jointly, *e. g.* they levy the necessary taxes for the county purposes; they purchase sites for and erect all county buildings that require an appropriation of over $500, and they elect, every other year, the county board of education.

Thus the people of the State, acting through a majority of their representatives, voluntarily surrendered their rights of local self-government and inaugurated a plan that approaches dangerously near an oligarchical form of government. This overthrow of local self-government was acquiesced in by a majority of the dominant political party, to save the people of the eastern section of the State from negro domination. As the question is now an open one in politics, it does not come within the scope of this paper to say whether the sacrifice has been worth the ends aimed at or not.

In the public school system, inaugurated in 1868 and modified in 1876, we find the most pernicious effects of this centralization of power in the hands of the dominant political party and the emasculation of local self-government. In the management of the public schools of the Northern and Northwestern States the people have taken a lively interest. Each county or township manages its own affairs, and has the right of increasing the regular appropriation for school purposes by local taxation, a most effective bond in uniting the people to the schools. Unfortunately both of these features are lacking in the system in operation in North Carolina. In the revolt against the form of government instituted in 1868, the men who formed the Constitutional Convention of 1876 allowed

---

[1] The county commissioners cannot appropriate over $500 for any purpose without the concurrence of a majority of the justices of the peace of the county.

the pendulum of local government to swing too far in the other direction. The school affairs of each county are in the hands of a county superintendent and a board of education. The board of education is elected by the board of county commissioners and the justices of the peace in joint session, and this board of education, in joint session with the board of county commissioners and justices of the peace, elects the county superintendent. This is the system, the wheel within a wheel, by which the dominant political party keeps control of the management of the public schools in every county in the State. Every vestige of local self-government has been removed. The school districts do not even have the privilege of electing their committees; they are appointed for them by the county board of education.[1] But as the public schools have suffered most from this system of centralization, it is more than probable that they will be the means by which the system will be entirely done away with or at least greatly modified. In 1889 an effort was made to amend the code so as to allow the voters of any township to vote a local tax upon themselves for the purpose of increasing their school fund; but unfortunately the law was so hampered and restricted that it has proved of no advantage to the rural districts. The State superintendent is still pressing upon the General Assembly the necessity of allowing any county or township to vote upon the question of taxing its citizens for school purposes.[2] These are straws which indicate the drift of opinion among the thinking classes. A change must come sooner or later. If it does not come in a political revolution—and we must remember that a single hostile legisla-

---

[1] Other duties of the board are to lay off their respective counties into two sets of school districts, the one for the white children and the other for the colored children. As the convenience of the two classes of residents must be consulted in laying off these districts, the two sets may or may not coincide. They apportion the county school fund among the districts, without discrimination in favor of or to the advantage of either race.

[2] Report for 1889 and 1890, pp. xii and xlix.

ture can do away with the whole present mode of local government—it will come when the people shall have acquired the right of increasing their school funds by local taxation. When once the barrier is broken citizens will not be slow to demand the other rights and privileges which they voluntarily surrendered in 1876.

W. A. WEBB.

NOTE ON NORTH CAROLINA.[1]

The Superintendent of Public Instruction of North Carolina, in his report for 1892, states that only fifteen cities in the State levy any special tax for schools. These cities embrace only 75,598 souls, or 4.6 per cent. of the population of the State. One reason given is that no vote can be had in any town relative to a special school tax without a petition of one-third of the freeholders; and the tax, if voted, allows only ten cents on one hundred dollars of property and thirty cents on polls. Even this must be approved by special act of the legislature.

The Superintendent strongly urges that the right to vote three times as much local tax as this be had in any township, city, town, or school district, on petition of any respectable number of freeholders. This entering wedge of local government is thus urged in the Superintendent's report:

"I know of no subject of taxation to which the people can be more safely trusted. If they vote taxes for schools, that fact means better schools, and consequently more safety to property and person as well as to our republican form of government. If communities have an opportunity to vote taxes for schools, and fail to do it, and so have poor schools as compared with other communities that have voted taxes, they will readily see the reason. Under such a provision, the different communities and neighborhoods would stimulate each other to better efforts, and much good would result."

---

[1] By the Editor.

II

LOCAL GOVERNMENT IN TENNESSEE.

Tennessee was originally a part of North Carolina, and the laws and local institutions were changed very little when the people west of the Alleghanies set up a government for themselves. In fact, there has been very little change since then.[1] The county and not the township system prevails. Every county is divided into civil districts, in each of which, unless it contain an incorporated town or city, there are elected two justices of the peace and a constable, besides the three school commissioners mentioned below. The justices of the peace, in addition to the judicial functions usually attaching to their office, compose the county court. This court, which controls the affairs of the county, meets on the first Monday of each month. When so meeting it is called the Quorum Court, but· is of little importance when compared with the Quarterly Court, which meets on the first Monday of January, April, July, and October. These four sessions of the county court are of the greatest importance and require the presence of the majority of the magistrates. The county court, at both its quarterly and monthly sessions, is presided over by the county judge, or, if there be no such officer elected in the county, the chairman of the county court. This officer is also the financial agent of the county.

The county court levies taxes, appropriates funds, controls public roads, looks after the poor of the county, builds bridges, jails, court-houses, and in other ways looks out for the welfare of the county. Within the limits fixed by statute the powers of this court are absolute.

At the January term the Quarterly Court hears the reports of the county judge or chairman of the county court, also of

---

[1] In consideration of the above fact this chapter is made very brief.

the turnpike inspectors, jail inspectors, and the superintendent of public schools. The commissioners of the poor also make their report and submit estimates for support of the poor, which the court appropriates in full or in part. This court elects the jail and turnpike inspectors, the commissioners of the poor, coroners, county surveyors, notaries public, and superintendent of public instruction. Road commissioners for each civil district are also appointed.

Special questions frequently are brought before this court, such as the building of bridges, court-houses, or any other buildings for the use of the county.

The powers of this court are restricted by the statutes. There are certain questions pertaining to the welfare of the people locally, concerning which the county court has no power to act, except by submitting the question to the people. For example, if a railroad were to ask for a subsidy the application would first come to the county court, which body would submit the question to the popular vote. Such questions as this are the only ones that ever come before the people.

The civil districts into which every county is divided have no significance whatever so far as local government is concerned. They are convenient as voting districts. Each district has two magistrates and a constable.

The civil district is also the school district. Three commissioners are elected in each district who have charge of the schools in that district. They build school-houses and employ teachers. The length of the school term is determined by the amount of money on hand. The people have no voice whatever in the control of the schools, except the influence of public sentiment. It must be said to the credit of the school commissioners—and not of the system—that the wish of the majority of the people is in most cases followed by the commissioners. It can be seen, though, at a glance that the people are helpless. The taxes levied for school purposes and the State fund are paid to the county treasurer, who prorates it to the several districts according to the scholastic population.

The superintendent of public instruction is elected biennially by the county court, and the State superintendent of public instruction is appointed by the Governor. The school commissioners manage the schools of the district.

Where the people of a civil district so desire, they may contribute money to the school fund so as to continue the school throughout the year. This is frequently done. And in this we have some approach to local government, but no local tax can be voted.

The county court controls the roads. A road commissioner is appointed by the court for each civil district in the county. This commissioner appoints the road overseers, and assigns those citizens subject to road duty to the several overseers.

In many Southern States there were introduced changes in the forms of local government just after the war,—in the days of the " carpet-bag rule." Such was not the case in Tennessee. The people, having never known anything else, believe in the existing system. As a rule the men in office have performed faithfully the duties imposed on them and for the best interests of the people whom they have represented. And thus they have made in a measure successful a system which under other circumstances might have been very burdensome.

F. P. TURNER.

NOTE ON TENNESSEE.[1]

When another constitutional convention assembles in Tennessee (and the sentiment in favor of it is rapidly growing), it is very likely that the power of local taxation will be largely extended. The following quotation, especially the closing sentence, taken from the report for 1891 of the State Superintendent of Public Instruction, Hon. W. R. Garrett, will prove interesting:

" Each county exercises county supervision through its superintendent, and is empowered through its county court

---

[1] By the Editor.

to supplement the revenues by a levy on polls, property and privileges, not to exceed the entire State tax for all purposes.

" Each district exercises supervision and control through its directors, who are invested with large discretionary powers in the use of the school fund and in the management of the schools. In the law as originally enacted, the district was empowered to levy an additional tax either to increase the length of the school term or to extend the course of study. This portion of the law was pronounced unconstitutional by the courts and was subsequently repealed. The constitution of the State does not permit a subordinate civil district to levy a tax. This power is limited to the General Assembly, the county court, and the authorities of the municipal corporation. Thus one important link in the general plan of the school system was broken, and the power of providing for the introduction of the higher branches was lost to the districts.

" In 1885 the General Assembly, at its extra session, repaired this broken link as far as the constitution would permit, and took the only step in its power to provide for local taxation. A law was passed empowering municipal corporations to levy additional taxes and to establish ' graded high schools.' This enactment was eminently wise and has led to important results. Graded high schools are now in efficient operation in all of the cities and in many of the towns. . . The successful operation of the corporation schools has produced the effect to make the country districts feel still more keenly the lack of the power of local taxation."

The county taxes for schools 1890-91 were $1,375,563.01, the city taxes in the fourteen cities reporting were $279,-649.51, and the receipts from all other sources, chiefly from State taxes, amounted to $329,582.92.

NOTE ON LOUISIANA.[1]

The material is not at hand for an account of the local government of Louisiana, but the great and perhaps necessary centralization of power in the State government there is illustrated in the school system.   The parish boards of education, which correspond to the county boards of other States, are chosen by the board of education, and the latter, consisting of one member from each congressional district, is appointed by the Governor.   The parish police jurors, corresponding to county commissioners elsewhere, may levy a parish tax, and incorporated towns have the powers, usual in this country, of town taxation.

The Legislature in 1891 gave expression to the growing demand for self-government in Louisiana by submitting to the vote of the people a constitutional amendment giving to every school district as well as to every parish the power to levy a school tax on vote of a majority of the taxpayers. Unfortunately, however, the proposed amendment was so worded, apparently by mistake, as to limit the amount that the parishes might raise even more than it increased the opportunities for a more local tax, and so was voted down by the friends of the schools.   A more carefully worded amendment may, in good time, be submitted to the people.   The State Superintendent, in his report for 1890-91, strongly urges local taxation for schools.

---

[1] By the Editor.

III.

LOCAL GOVERNMENT IN ALABAMA.

The State is divided into 68 counties, varying from four hundred to sixteen hundred square miles. The county is a body corporate, of which the county commissioners are trustees, and as such body corporate it can sue or be sued, buy, sell and own property and issue bonds. The county officers consist of a Judge of Probate, Clerk of the Circuit Court, Sheriff, Tax Collector, Tax Assessor, Treasurer, Coroner, County Superintendent of Education, and four Commissioners. All of these are elected by popular vote, except that in forty-five counties the County Superintendent of Education is appointed by the State Superintendent. In some counties the commissioners are elected from districts, in others from the county at large.

The Probate Judge is, *ex officio*, president of the Court of County Commissioners, but has no vote except in case of a tie, which is very frequent on account of the number of the commissioners (4). This court has complete control of the affairs of the county, and its powers are specified in the code. It has original jurisdiction over the change, discontinuance, or establishment of (public) roads, bridges, causeways and ferries within the county.[1] Bridges are kept up by a special tax, or by moneys appropriated from the general fund. Roads are kept up in the following manner: Apportioners are appointed who class the roads and divide them into sections, appoint overseers for each section, and assign to each a quota of hands. Every male over 18 and under 45 who is free from physical deformity is subject to not more than 10 days' duty on the public roads each year. In the municipal

---

[1] Code, §825.

corporations a street tax is generally substituted for this service. When a new road is to be established, the court appoints surveyors to select the route, whereupon the land is condemned, assessed, and paid for by the county.

The county court has authority—

1. To control the property of the county.

2. To levy a general tax for general, and a special tax for special county purposes.

3. To examine, settle and allow all accounts and claims chargeable against the county.

4. To examine and audit the accounts of all officers having the care, management, collection or disbursement of county funds.

5. To provide for the support of the poor.

6. To punish for contempt.

7. To exercise such other powers as are given to it.

The State tax is the same all over the State, but the county tax varies in the different counties and in the same county from year to year, but the State and county tax together rarely exceed one per cent., and often fall below three-fifths of one per cent. Special taxes are not often levied, except to keep up bridges and pay interest on county bonds.

In almost every county a poor-house has been provided. It is generally in charge of some person who receives a certain amount per month per capita for supporting and taking care of the poor. The house is often inferior and not always well kept, but is generally situated in the country, where fuel costs nothing and pure air is plentiful.

This county court also has control of all stock-law questions. A large portion of the State is woodland, and it is often found preferable to inclose the land devoted to agriculture and let stock run at large on the rest. The stock-law provides that the landowners of any section shall decide by ballot, voting by acres, whether they want to be compelled to fence their arable land or not. If the majority of acres are cast for stock-law, which means no fences, then, at the discretion of the commissioners, it is declared that stock cannot run at large in that region except during certain months. In some sections of the State the stock-law obtains entirely, in others not at all, and between these two extremes bitter contests often occur.

The county is subdivided by the commissioners' court into precincts or voting districts. These are merely divisions for political purposes and are not corporations at all. Each precinct is allowed to elect two justices of the peace and a constable, who is the executive officer. Beyond this the precincts can do nothing. They can tax themselves for nothing. Only the county commissioners can impose a tax, and that equally over the whole county, and only for county purposes. Precincts are merely election districts, and the county commissioners may provide one or two voting places in each as they think the convenience of the electors requires. The constitution gives the Governor power to appoint one notary public in each beat, who shall be *ex officio* justice of the peace. This was done in order that every beat, especially where the negroes predominate, might have at least one white justice.

The classification of municipal corporations into city, town, and village is merely a distinction in name, there being no difference at all in the government of the three. Every municipal corporation within the State is governed either by a special charter or by the general charter provided in the code. Only the smaller municipal corporations are governed by the charter provided by the code, the larger ones and a great many of the smaller ones having obtained special charters. We shall not attempt to discuss the latter class, but will consider only the former. In the charter provided by the code, the executive officer is called the Intendant; in some of the special charters he is still called Intendant, in others, Mayor.

The incorporation of towns of more than one hundred inhabitants is provided for by the code. If a petition signed by more than twenty adults be filed with the judge of probate, asking for the incorporation of a certain place, he must at

once give notice and order an election to determine whether
the majority wish the place incorporated or not. The vote is
" Corporation " or " No Corporation." If " Corporation "
wins, the place is incorporated under the general charter provided by the code. The executive of the corporation is the
marshal, and the other officers are the intendant and five
councilmen, who have power—

To pass such laws and regulations as may be necessary for
their own government not contrary to law.

To prevent and remove nuisances.

To tax, license, regulate and restrain shows and amuse-
ments.

To restrain and prohibit disorderly houses, disorderly conduct, gaming, and breaches of the peace.

To establish watches and patrols.

To license, regulate and restrain the selling of spirituous,
malt and vinous liquors within the corporate limits.

To establish and regulate markets.

To license and regulate drays.

To purchase, sell, and own real and personal property.

To exercise such other powers as may be given them by
law.

The constitution provides that the State tax shall not
exceed three-fourths of one per cent., and also prohibits counties from levying a tax greater than one-half of one per cent.,
except for some special . reason, as the erection of a court-
house; and municipal corporations also have their tax rate
limited to one-half of one per cent. (except Mobile, three-
fourths of one per cent.) This applies to all municipal corporations, whether under the general or a special charter.

A license on bar-rooms not exceeding $500 may be im-
posed by municipal corporations, and a small license on other
businesses, which money is to be expended in keeping up the
corporation, and may be spent for schools, if the council so
prefer. We do not attempt to say how many city councils
expend this tax for the support of schools; our personal
knowledge extends to only one; there may be others. Of

course in those towns that have public schools supported
by the town funds, these licenses are expended for schools
indirectly, since they go into the general fund from which the
school fund is appropriated.

The public school system of Alabama is under the control of the State Superintendent, assisted by a county superintendent in each county, township superintendents or trustees in each township, and the superintendents of the special
school districts.

Every township and every incorporated town or city
having 3000 inhabitants constitutes a separate school district,
and each of them in all matters connected with public
schools is under a township superintendent or trustees. Each
township or other school district in its corporate capacity
may hold real and personal property, and the business of corporations, in relation to public schools and school lands, is
managed by the township or district superintendent.

Under this provision townships may hold property, but no
special tax can be levied for the support of schools. In the
Cullman (special) school districts as first organized an attempt
was made to levy a special tax for the support of schools, but
the Supreme Court declared it unconstitutional.

The money, then, for the support of schools (except in
special school districts) must come from the State and from
voluntary contributions, usually in the form of tuition. The
general school fund is, in round numbers, $650,000 per
annum,—$350,000 from special legislative appropriation,
$150,000 from interest on the sixteenth section fund and
other sources, and $150,000 from a poll tax. Every male
between 21 and 45 pays a poll tax of $1.50, which is applied
to the support of schools in the district and for the race to
which he belongs. The remaining $500,000 is distributed
over the State per capita, the distribution being based on a
school census taken every two years by the district superintendents. In taking the census the superintendents count all
the school children (between seven and twenty-one), whether
they are enrolled on a school register or not, or whether the
district has a school or not.

The State Superintendent is general overseer of all the schools in the State, and is required to visit each county once a year if practicable. He apportions the State funds and keeps accounts with those who disburse them. He is required to study the school systems of other States, and make such suggestions to the Governor or Legislature as he thinks best. He makes an annual report to the Governor. The county superintendent is elected in twenty-three counties and appointed by the State Superintendent in forty-five. He has general oversight of the public schools in the county. He disburses all the funds, except in special districts, and is responsible to the State Superintendent for all moneys sent to himself. His pay is $75 and two per cent. of all moneys paid out.

The township superintendent is appointed by the county superintendent. Each township has a superintendent (except those counties which, by special act, have three trustees instead of a superintendent for each township, with identically the same powers and duties as a township superintendent), and he has immediate control of the public schools in his township. He receives no compensation, and his duties and powers as laid down in the code are as follows:

He may establish one or more schools in each township for each race, the co-education of the races being prohibited by the constitution. He is required to call annually a meeting of the parents and guardians in his township and consult with them as to the number and location of schools, "with a view to subserve their wishes, interests and convenience." In this way he is to determine the number and duration of schools, their location, and what per cent. of the public funds each is to receive. The township superintendent is not merely the executive officer of this meeting, but he has power to disregard its instructions altogether. Should the people dislike what he does, they have the right to appeal to the county superintendent. Such a meeting must be advertised for ten days by posted notices in at least three places, setting forth the business to be discussed at said meeting. If the parents

and guardians fail to attend such a meeting, as is generally the case, the township superintendent performs such
duties as, in such cases, are required of him. In locating
public schools, township superintendents "shall have due
regard to such communities as will supplement the general
district fund," and as will provide houses. There are, out-
side of the special school districts, very few schools supported entirely by public funds, and the township having no
power to tax itself, the "supplement" must come from private sources. The public fund is about $1.40 per capita per
annum. This would not sustain the public schools more
than a month if all of the children were to attend. But half of
them rarely attend, and in a good many districts, especially
where the negroes are numerous, summer schools, entirely
public, are maintained at least three months. All the
schools that amount to anything are private (except in special school districts). A community will employ a teacher
and allow him to charge tuition, which varies from one to
five dollars per month. The township superintendent will
locate that school as one of the supplemented public schools,
and set aside for it such amount of the public funds as is
equal to the *pro rata* share of all the children who live near
and are likely to attend that school. This money the teacher
prorates among the children who attend school, and deducts
each one's share from his tuition bill. It is generally the case
that not more than one-half, frequently less than one-fourth,
of the children of the community attend the school, and these
funds reduce the tuition bills considerably. It is an unde-
cided point whether a child who refuses to pay tuition can
attend such a school. Many think that he can. The question often comes up, but has never been decided, so far as I
know. In small towns and villages little attention is paid to
the public funds. In most places one, frequently two, good
schools are kept for nine or ten months a year, and the public
funds are so small that little is said of them. It is only in the
country districts (and this is most of the State, over 75 per
cent. of the people living there) that these funds are of much

benefit. Then in the summer and winter, rarely spring and autumn, schools of three months' duration depend entirely upon public funds. The teachers receive from twenty to thirty-five dollars a month, and are generally young men or girls from eighteen to twenty-one who have nothing else to do during the summer or winter. In most rural districts the people are generally too poor to pay tuition, and this little schooling is all that their children receive. This is especially the case among the negroes. Many who are able to do so educate their children at the neighboring village school. This is expensive, as both board and tuition must be paid. It will be a long time yet before Alabama has a system of public schools that will meet all her wants. The chief drawback to the establishment of such a system is the presence of the negro and his legal equality with the whites. The nearest approach which we have to an adequate system is in the case of special school districts.

Eighteen special school districts have been created by special act of the legislature. Most of these are co-extensive with the corporate limits of the towns or cities which they embrace. Mobile county and the Cullman districts, embracing a large part of Cullman county, are the chief exceptions. Mobile county had a system of public schools at the time of the adoption of the present constitution, and in it this county is excepted from the control of the general school laws. While all these special districts are created by different acts of the legislature, they somewhat resemble each other. Each receives its share of the general school fund, and is given power to set aside a fund from the general revenue of the town, which is identical with the special school district, for the support of schools. In each district, separate schools for each race must be maintained. In some, a board of school commissioners is created; in others, the city council is made such a board. Schools, when co-extensive with the city, are generally supported by moneys from the general fund, which is made up of taxes, licenses, and fines; in other districts, by special tax. The entire tax for all purposes in no city can

exceed one-half of one per cent., except in Mobile and Birmingham; in Mobile by permission of the constitution, in
Birmingham by amendment to the constitution. The city
public schools are very good and give general satisfaction. It
is by the creation of special school districts that an improvement in the school system is most likely to come, and it will
come first in districts having few negroes.

W. F. NIX.

NOTE ON ALABAMA.[1]

In " History of Education in Alabama "[2] it is estimated
that the patrons of the public schools supplement the public
funds by about one-third in order to secure better schools.
This valuable monograph also shows that the constitution
has greatly interfered, even in special school districts, with the
growing efforts to supplement State school funds by local
taxes. Probably this will be changed when Alabama holds
another constitutional convention.

Ten special school districts made returns to the State
Superintendent of Public Education for 1891-2. The returns
for Mobile were incomplete. The other nine districts, with
a total school enrolment of 3,718, and an average attendance
of 2,576, appropriated $43,811.87 from local revenues to sup-
plement State aid, tuition fees and other receipts of $11,553.40.
Local government and taxation are less developed in Alabama than in most of the Southern States.

---

[1] By the Editor.
[2] Published by U. S. Bureau of Education, 1889.

IV

THE LOCAL INSTITUTIONS OF GEORGIA.

The peculiar considerations which led to the establishment of Georgia, the unprecedented charter under which it was founded, and the character of the people invited to its borders, all give to it a unique place among the original thirteen colonies. While the troubles of the early settlers with the Indians, by which the colony was well-nigh depopulated, the changes wrought by the Revolutionary and Civil wars, combined with the influence of her sister States, have done much to efface some deep marks of distinction, still we can trace with more or less certainty the influence of the early days upon her later history, literature and institutions. The threads of this influence are tangled, broken and sometimes lost, and yet a glance at Georgia's colonial government may not prove unprofitable in a study of her present local institutions.

The history of Georgia as a ward of the Trustees covers the twenty years between 1732 and 1752. Three motives led to the foundation of the colony:

1. To afford an asylum for the indigent of Europe.
2. To aid in the conversion of the Indians.
3. To serve as a bulwark to South Carolina against the threatened invasion of the Spaniards from Florida.

It was the first and second considerations which were most prominent in the minds of the Trustees. They allowed themselves no salary, and carefully arranged the charter so that neither they nor their heirs could derive any benefit from the scheme. The historian Dr. Stevens says: " It was the first colony ever founded by charity. New England had been settled by Puritans who fled thither for conscience sake, New York by a company of merchants and adventurers in search of gain, Maryland by Papists retiring from Protestant intol-

erance, Virginia by ambitious cavaliers, Carolina by the
scheming and visionary Shaftesbury, but Georgia was planted
by the hand of benevolence and reared into being by the
hands of disinterested charity."

The primary scheme of government was simple enough.
The following officers were appointed from among the emi-
grants for the new town, Savannah: Three bailiffs, two tithing-
men, a recorder, two constables, and eight conservators of the
peace. A court of judicature known as the "Town Court"
was erected, in which all things happening or arising in the
province were to be tried according to the laws of England
and those established in Georgia. This court was composed
of the three bailiffs and the recorder acting as clerk. Only
freeholders were allowed to serve on the jury. The Town
Court of Savannah had no connection with a higher, but was
itself supreme. While Oglethorpe was in Savannah, the
power of the bailiffs was merged in him, but his residence was
an intermittent one. The result which might have been
expected to flow from the folly of conferring such civil and
judicial powers upon the bailiffs was not slow to appear.
Referring to this, one writer says: "Having never before
held the staff of office, they became intoxicated with their
elevation, and used their little brief authority like so many
autocrats in miniature."

This plan of government proving unsatisfactory, a committee was appointed by the Trustees for remodeling the government and establishing a constitution to be administered by
a president and several assistants. The province was accordingly divided into two counties, Savannah and Frederica.
Over each was to be a president and four assistants, who were
to constitute the civil and judicial tribunal of their respective
departments. Oglethorpe was to exercise civil and military
control over the entire colony, thus obviating the rivalries,
jealousies and collisions which would have arisen between the
two counties. Both counties united under one executive, the
president and his assistants, to hold four courts each year in
Savannah.

An annual representative Assembly, to be held in Savannah, was provided for. This Assembly was to meet in Savannah at the most convenient time of the year, the meeting not to continue over a month. Every town, village or district where ten families were settled in the province was to be allowed one deputy, and where there were thirty families, two deputies; Savannah was to have four. The power to make laws being entirely in the hands of the Trustees, the Assembly could only act as an advisory body. Besides other information demanded of the deputy, was the unique requirement that "he deliver in writing an account of the mulberry trees (properly fenced) standing on each plantation in his district." The failure of Georgia to make a silk-raising State was certainly not due to the lack of encouragement and even pressure on the part of both the Assembly and Trustees. After June, 1751, no person was to be chosen as deputy who had not one hundred mulberry trees planted and properly fenced on every fifty acres of land he possessed, and after June 24, 1753, no person who had not also at least one female in his family instructed in the art of reeling silk.

There are four clearly defined periods in the development of the local institutions of Georgia, which might be considered:

1. As a ward of the Trustees.
2. As a Royal Province.
3. As a slave State from 1777 to the emancipation of the negro.
4. From the adoption of the constitution of 1868 until the present time.

Resisting the temptation of glancing at the institutions of each period as we have at those of the first, we shall hasten to the local government of to-day.

The county is the unit of local government. Each county is divided into militia districts according to its territory and population. The largest counties have six representatives in the lower house, and the smallest counties, one.

The officers of the county are Ordinary, Treasurer, Sheriff, Tax Collector, Tax Receiver, Surveyor, and Clerk. These officers are elected by vote of the qualified voters of the county, and, with the exception of the ordinary, who is elected for four years, hold office for two years. According to the constitution of 1877 the county officers were made uniform throughout the State.

The chief officer is the Ordinary. His position is one of much power and responsibility. Courts of Ordinary have the right to exercise original, exclusive, and general jurisdiction of the following nature:

1. Probate of wills.

2. Granting and relieving letters testamentary and of administration.

3. Controversies of executorship and administration.

4: Sale and disposition of property of deceased persons.

5. The appointment and removal of guardians, and in all controversies as to the right of guardians.

6. All matters relating to deceased persons, idiots, and lunatics.

When sitting for county purposes the Ordinary has original and exclusive jurisdiction over the following:

1. In directing and controlling all the property of the county.

2. In levying a tax for county purposes.

3. In establishing, altering or abolishing all roads, bridges, or ferries.

4. In establishing and changing election and militia districts.

. 5. In supplying vacancies in county offices and in ordering elections to fill them.

6. In settling all claims against the county.

7. In auditing all accounts of officers having county moneys in charge.

8. In making such rules and regulations for the support of the county poor, and for county police as are in accordance with the laws of the county.

The above, though far from including all the powers of the
Ordinary, will serve to give some idea of the extent of his
authority. This concentration of power in the Ordinary
forms the most distinctive and unique feature in the local
government of the State. It is interesting to trace his title,
so to speak, and see when so much authority was placed
in his hands. The constitution of 1821 provided for the election in each county of five justices of the Inferior Court. In
the code we find this provision, which is the first intimation
of an Ordinary: " When the inferior court is sitting for ordinary purposes it shall be known only as sitting for ordinary
purposes, and the clerk shall be known as clerk of the Ordinary."

The court established according to the constitution of 1851
is styled the Court of Ordinary and the incumbent as Ordinary.

According to the constitution of 1865 the powers of the
Court of Ordinary and Probate were invested in the Ordinary elected every four years and commissioned by the Governor. He was empowered to issue citations, grant tempor-
ary letters of administration, and to grant marriage license.
His powers were still, however, but a tithe of what they were
to become.

According to the constitution of 1868 the Inferior Court
was abolished and most of the powers of the five justices
were given to the Ordinary. Almost every legislature con-
ferred new powers upon the Ordinary. He became more
and more the center of all authority in the county.

The Ordinary, we thus see, is an outgrowth of the old country justices, but a plant of very different kind. Several safeguards have been thrown around the officer. After his election the Ordinary must be qualified by the judge of the Superior Court, he must give a bond of not less than one thousand dollars, and all his acts are open to the scrutiny of the
grand jury.

There is nothing about the other county offices that needs
special mention.

The censors of the county are the grand jurors. All males above 21 and under 60, who are deemed upright and intelligent citizens, are qualified to act as grand jurors. It is the duty of the Ordinary, together with the clerk of the Superior Court and three commissioners appointed by the judge of the Superior Court, to meet at the court-house the first Monday in June biennially, to select jurors from the books of the tax collector and make out tickets with the names, thus selected, on them. These tickets are placed in a box with two separate departments numbered "one" and "two." This box is locked up and sealed by the judge, given over to the clerk, and the key is entrusted to the sheriff. The judge of the Superior Court, at the end of each term, causes to be drawn from number "one" in open court not less than eighteen nor more than thirty names to serve as grand jurors at the next term of court. All of these names are deposited in number "two." When all the names have been withdrawn from "one," the process is reversed. No name. can be thrown out of the box unless the juror is dead, removed out of the county or otherwise disqualified by law. As the judge is appointed by the Governor, and the jury commissioners by the judge, it is possible for the jury to be confined to one political party, viz., the one represented by the Governor. The result has been to exclude the negro largely from jury service. The following are some of the duties of the men so carefully selected:

From term to term of the Superior Court they are to inspect and examine the offices, papers, books, and records of the Clerk of the Superior Court, Ordinary, and Treasurer. They are to examine the list of voters and to present any illegal voter for violation of the law. They are to inquire into and report on the financial condition of the county, to correct mistakes in Tax Receivers' returns, to present the Road Commissioners for neglect of duty, to select the County Board of Education, to inquire into the record of the prisoners, and to examine and approve the reports of the county officers.

There has been recently much legislation upon public roads. Whatever may be the perfection secured in the laws, the effect is not yet visible in the roads themselves.

According to an act of 1818, the Ordinary is required to lay his county off into road districts and apportion the roads and hands so that the burden of road duties shall fall equally upon all. He is also to appoint biennially three commissioners for each district. It is the duty of these commissioners to appoint overseers for road hands in their district, to properly apportion the various roads and hands, and to furnish each overseer with a list of the roads and hands under his charge. They are to hold a court after the road-working to hear all cases of default or other violation of the road laws. It is their duty to inspect the public roads, bridges, and ferries within their districts, and to exercise a general supervision over the overseers in their district and to fine them for neglect of duty. A person appointed road commissioner is required to serve, and if he neglects his business he may be reported by a member of the grand jury and fined not less than fifty dollars. The only compensation is exemption from jury, patrol, militia and other road duties.

When application is made for a new road or the alteration of an old one, the Ordinary appoints three commissioners to investigate the advisability of granting the request. If they recommend that it be granted, the Ordinary posts a notice of the application for 30 days, at the end of which time the road is granted, provided no objection is made. The code has provided since 1818 that the public roads must be laid out the nearest and best way, but there is no way of enforcing the law and it has always remained a dead letter.

All male inhabitants between the ages of sixteen and fifty are subject to road duty; exemptions are made in the case of licensed ministers, teachers and pupils in schools and colleges, public mills, ferries, etc, white persons in charge of railroad trains, officers of the county, State or United States, members of the County Board of Education and others. Tools or horses may be substituted for the labor of persons. The result of so many exemptions is that road duties are rarely performed by the wealthy or influential planters.

The public schools of the State are in the hands of a State Board of Education composed of the Governor, Attorney-General, Secretary of State, Comptroller-General, and State School Commissioner. The latter officer is appointed by the Governor.

Each county forms a school district, and is placed in charge of a County Board of Education. This county board is composed of five freeholders, appointed usually by the grand jury, but in some few counties secured by popular election.

This board elects one of its own members as County School Commissioner. The compensation allowed the other members of the board is exemption from road, jury, and militia duties, but the commissioner may be given in addition such salary as the board may vote him, provided he is never paid more than $3.00 per day for time employed in the discharge of his official duties.

The County School Commissioner must examine all applicants for license to teach. He is to serve as the medium of communication between the State School Commissioner and his subordinates. He is expected to visit each school in his county twice during the year, an expectation which, it may be remarked, is seldom, if ever, realized. The code also provides that he shall every four years take a complete census of the youths of his county, noting the number of white and colored children. He is also required to report annually to the grand jury, and to place his books before them for examination.

Admission to the public schools of the State is gratuitous to all children between the ages of six and eighteen. White and colored children cannot attend the same school.

The code still contains the somewhat curious provision that the school revenue shall be apportioned to each county upon the basis of the aggregate of youths between six and eighteen *and all Confederate soldiers under thirty years old.* The school fund consists of the poll tax; tax on liquors, shows and exhibitions; dividends upon railroad stocks owned by the State; all moneys received by the agricultural department for the inspection of fertilizers in excess of what is needed to defray the expenses of that department; the net amount arising from the hire of convicts, and such other funds as may be appropriated from time to time by the legislature.

It is provided that equal advantages shall be given so far as possible to both races, a provision which has been carefully observed, notwithstanding the fact that the whole management of educational matters has been almost entirely in the hands of the whites.

According to an act of 1890, teachers' institutes have been established in every county in the State. Every teacher is required to attend an institute for at least one week during the year.

An act of Sept. 16, 1891, provides that a local tax to supplement the State school tax may be levied in any county where a county school system is not already in existence. After two successive juries have recommended this supplementary tax, the Ordinary orders an election, which is to be held under the same rules as the usual elections of the county. If two-thirds of the voters qualified to vote at this election declare for local taxation, the Ordinary notifies the County Board of Education, who in turn fix the rate of taxation, which is not to exceed one-fourth of one per cent. of the taxable property of the county.

Any county in which a county school system is already in existence, but where the funds, in the opinion of the County Board of Education, are insufficient, may obtain the benefits of this act by complying with the provisions. An incorporated town or city in the county having a school system of its own sustained by local taxation is not allowed to vote in this election, and the property in the town, of course, is not subject to the county school tax. In counties where there is a registration law, two-thirds of the voters on the last registration list must be secured, and in counties where there is no such law the same proportion of the citizens whose names appear upon the books of the Tax Collector as having paid their tax must vote for the local tax to carry the law.

This provision that two-thirds of the qualified voters, instead of two-thirds of the qualified votes cast, should be necessary, the requiring the recommendation of two successive grand juries, most if not all of whom are freeholders, and finally giving the County Board of Education, all of whom are landowners, the right of fixing the rate, all show that local taxation for county schools is still in the hands of the property owners. This act of 1891 is, however, an important step forward in local government.

F. S. Brockman.

Note on Georgia.[1]

A steadily increasing number of cities and incorporated towns are possessed of the right of local taxation for school purposes. Thirteen cities, three counties and ten incorporated towns are thus reported by the State Superintendent in his report for 1890, while in another part of the same report he mentions the names of three other counties and eleven towns that have lately received from the legislature this privilege of local taxation for school purposes. During 1886-1890 inclusive this privilege was granted to twenty-two towns and three counties and has been acted upon by nearly all.

Note on Mississippi.[2]

The county governing body is composed of a member called a supervisor, chosen for four years from each one of five districts. In thirty-two enumerated counties where in 1890 there were 512,276 blacks and only 207,323 whites, or 71 blacks to every 29 whites, each supervisor must possess real estate worth $250. In the remaining forty-three counties which have 337,518 whites and 232,473 colored, or 59 whites to every 41 colored, the supervisor must possess $100 worth

---

[1] By the Editor.   [2] By the Editor.

of real estate. Each supervisor must also give bond equal to
five per cent. of the previous year's taxes raised in the county
for State and county purposes. The board of supervisors
levies and disburses the county revenue and manages nearly
all of the county affairs.

There are only two important kinds of government within
the county,—the special school district, and the incorporated
municipality. Of the latter type are 19 cities of from 2,000
to 13,500 inhabitants each, or a total of 85,490, and some of
the 187 small cities and villages, of which the 116 making
returns to the last census, and supposably the largest, had
63,741 inhabitants, or an average of 550. Villages of under
300 inhabitants can levy only a four-mill tax on the dollar.
Those over 300 and under 5,000 can levy a six-mill tax for
general expenses and as much more for general improve-
ments. Places over 5,000 inhabitants can levy a twenty-mill
tax for the two objects stated above, or for schools. There
are four places in the State over 6,000 and with a total population of 40,756.

The other type of local government below the county is the
special school district. In these districts, of which there were
43 in 1891, 35 having been organized since 1888, there was an
average attendance of 14,963 pupils in 1891, or 7.6 per cent.
of the attendance of the entire State.

Any place of over 750 inhabitants can become a special
school district, in which case the mayor and aldermen select
the trustees. These trustees control the school and must
keep it open seven months a year, or three months more than
is required in other parts of the State, but they cannot levy a
tax exceeding three mills without the consent of a majority of
the taxpayers of the municipality.

In the rest of the State the County Superintendent of Education, who is appointed in most counties by the State Board
of Education, but elected in a few instances, fixes the salaries
of teachers and appoints them, following any recommenda-
tions, if given, of the district trustees. The latter are elected
annually by the school patrons, and must be able to read and

write. The county school board, consisting of one from each
of the five supervisors' districts, is appointed by the county
superintendent, subject to the approval of the board of supervisors. This Board of Education, among other duties, defines
boundaries and locates school-houses.

NOTE ON SOUTH CAROLINA.[1]

As stated in the introduction, local government in South
Carolina was treated in another monograph in these Historical Studies (Vol. I., No. 12), prepared in 1883 by Dr. B.
J. Ramage. At that time, save in a few towns and cities,
there was no important political subdivision of the county,
and even the amount of tax for various purposes that the
elective county commissioners could raise was fixed by the
legislature. In school matters, the Governor appointed the
State Board of Examiners. The latter appointed the county
board of examiners, who in turn divided the county into
school districts and appointed three trustees for each, but had
no power of county taxation for schools. The nearest approach to the town-meeting or *referendum* was in the power
of these trustees to " call meetings of the people of the district for consultation in regard to the school interests thereof."

On December 24, 1888, a great extension of local government in South Carolina was made by a law providing for
local taxation for school purposes in any school district so
desiring. The conditions are, first, that a majority of the resident freeholders must petition for it. Then the school trustees call a meeting of all who return $100 worth of real or
personal property for taxation. This meeting elects a chairman and secretary, and can levy a tax not exceeding two
mills on the dollar and appropriate it " to such school purposes as a majority present shall see fit." The county treasurer collects the tax, which is expended in the district; but
" each taxpayer, when he pays any tax for school purposes
voted under the provisions of this act, shall have the right to

---

[1] By the Editor.

designate to which school in his district he wishes the money paid by him to go," and the money must be so expended. If there is no such designation of the tax, the money is spent like the other funds of the district.

I suppose the school meeting merely appropriates the tax levy for a certain class of expenses, such as teachers' salaries, school buildings, apparatus, etc., and then the taxpayer can designate further the school. This power would probably be much appreciated by the whites in a county like Beaufort, where there were in 1890 only 2,695 whites to 31,424 colored, or Berkely, where there were 7,687 whites to 47,741 colored persons, who were presumably much smaller taxpayers.

This law is a strong entering wedge for local government. Many towns with limited powers of local government and some cities are yearly incorporated.

Twenty-one of the thirty-five counties of the State report to the State Superintendent of Education for 1891-2 that special, *i. e.* local, school taxes in their counties amounted to $57,329.64, or 15.2 per cent. of the total receipts for school purposes. There have been created in the State since 1877, by special acts of the legislature, eighty-six special school districts, aside from the separate school districts provided for by the general law of 1888. Of these eighty-six, twenty-one have the right to levy a three-mill tax, four a four-mill tax, and five a five-mill tax. Nearly all the rest, like the separate districts, can levy a two-mill tax.

Note on Florida.[1]

The chief development of local government in Florida, as elsewhere, is connected with schools. By virtue of a law of June 8, 1889, it is provided that, on petition of one-fourth of the voters in any election district or town, a vote must be taken relative to the formation of a school district with three elective trustees therein. In any school district thus created the County Board of Education, when petitioned to do so,

---

[1] By the Editor.

and when it deems the action advisable, has an election in the district to determine the propriety of a special local tax for school purposes. At this election a majority of all those paying real or personal taxes can vote a tax not exceeding three mills for school purposes. In districts where the trustees are not elected, those nominated by the patrons are usually appointed. The patrons of a school often hold an election for the choice of a teacher when not appointed by the trustees. The County Board of Education, consisting of three members, who locate and maintain the schools and levy a tax of three to five mills, are nominated by the State Superintendent of Education and confirmed by the State Board of Education, which is an elective body.

The five county commissioners, who administer most of the affairs of the county, are appointed by the Governor and Senate, but the people elect the County Superintendent of Education and the assessor. In the election districts assistant assessors may be appointed by the county commissioners if the legislature so orders.

Three hundred or more voters in a place are sufficient for incorporation as a city, and twenty-five male inhabitants likewise are sufficient for an incorporated town. Both have a mayor and council, who have the power to pass ordinances and to levy a tax not exceeding one per cent. for schools, streets, the poor, infirm, insane, and for many other purposes. The tax for interest, water works and fire protection may exceed one per cent. About 130,000, or one-third of the population of the State, according to the census of 1890, lived in cities and villages. There were three of these places with from 11,750 to 18,080 inhabitants, twenty-three from 1,000 to 5,600, and seventy-five from 54 to 1,000. The number of these small places enjoying local government—for a considerable proportion are incorporated—must be taken into account in considering the local government of the State.

V.

· TEXAS.

In the latter part of the year 1684 La Salle established the first European colony within the present limits of Texas. This colony lived only a short time. In 1686 Mexico took nominal military possession of the country, and five years later Don Domingo Teran was appointed Governor of Coahuila and Texas, with instructions to establish agricultural colonies in the southern and most fertile sections of the territory. This assumption of sovereignty by Mexico did not cause France to relinquish her claim to Texas, nor did France recognize the Spanish treaty of 1803 with the United States as binding, but continued a spasmodic controversy until the treaty of Guadalupe Hidalgo, in 1848. The republic of Mexico prescribed military government for the new settlements as they were established, and this form of general and local government, which was in course of time widened and elaborated to suit the demands of the colonists, prevailed until 1821, when the Mexican nation was declared "free and independent of the Spanish government and every other forever."

Under the constitution of the United Mexican States, the provinces of Coahuila and Texas were made a State co-ordinate in internal administrative powers with the other constituent States of the confederation. The form of the State government was representative, popular and federal, and like the government of the United States was divided into three branches, namely, the legislative, executive, and the judicial. The government of the confederation was similar to that of the United States in that its powers were enumerated, giving to the States all powers and rights not expressly granted to the central government. The confederation was sovereign as to all proper international relations, while the States were sovereign as to general police powers and local taxation. A State constitution for Coahuila and Texas was framed at Saltillo, and proclaimed March 11, 1827, and in this constitution it is declared 'that the "sovereignty of the State resides originally and essentially in the mass of individuals who compose it," the form and substance of such powers being defined and designated by the constitution of the State. At the formation of this constitution the State was divided into three departments, namely, Bexar, Monclova, and Parras, and power was given Congress to alter and readjust this division to suit the advantages of the different sections.

The State was divided into ayuntamientos, local subdivisions of State government, somewhat like our county at present, as to its functions of government. The ayuntamiento district was divided into electoral municipal assemblies, like our present election precinct, but more to suit the convenience of the scattered communities than in accordance with geographical surveys. These primary juntas, or municipal assemblies, were composed of all qualified voters residing within the specified limits. The elections were held on Sunday and the following Monday, the session lasting four hours each day. At these times electors were chosen to meet in conjunction with electors from other municipal assemblies and vote for members of Congress, the Governor, and other high officers of State. The ayuntamiento was a board of officers elected by means of electoral municipal assemblies to establish and direct police powers and regulations and general internal government for the towns and communities of the State. Congress could, upon proper application and sufficient demand shown, establish ayuntamientos, and in the enabling act would designate the number of officers, alcaldes or presidents, who had power to exercise both legislative and judicial functions somewhat like the mayor of some of our Southern cities. Syndics having powers similar to our modern city councillors, and aldermen similar to the modern Board of Public Works, were next in power to the alcaldes.

The alcaldes were to be renewed yearly, of the aldermen half were renewed every year, and also the syndics, if there were more than two, but if only one, he was changed every year. Each ayuntamiento would make out annually a full report of its financial and industrial conditions and forward to the Chief of Department, who would report to the Governor or Congress, and the ayuntamiento would publish a copy of the same in a public place. The ayuntamiento was the local unit of taxation as well as of civil government. The tax lists were made out by the ayuntamiento, and the assessments were collected by agents of its own appointment. Ten per cent. of the tax was applied to the current expenses of the ayuntamiento, to pay the tax commissioners and other local functionaries, and the remainder went to the State.

In 1836, we find the English and American colonists tired of Spanish and Catholic rule. By strong exertion they threw off Mexican allegiance, proclaimed their independence, and established a provisional government, which was superseded, in a few months, by a permanent republic. The constitution of the republic was, to a large extent, a copy of the United States plan of individual statehood. The church was cut loose from political government; religious qualifications were no longer necessary for eligibility to the franchise and office. The electoral system of voting was supplanted by the popular ballot. The Legislature was divided into two branches, a House of Representatives and a Senate, the members of both being elected by popular vote in districts determined by due apportionment of the full population. The executive was elected by popular vote. The State was imperfectly divided into counties, and in each county was established a county court and such justices' courts as Congress thought proper. In this change the strict form of Continental government and the çivil law sink beneath the greater liberality of the United States government and the English common law. In 1845 the Republic of Texas ceased to be an independent sovereignty, by being admitted as a State into the United States of America. The old constitution and laws of the republic needed only slight modifications to meet the requirements of the constitution and laws of the United States.

At present the county is the distinctive unit of local self-government. Some of the counties are still very large. The counties organized since 1879 contain not less than seven nor more than nine hundred square miles, and all counties that shall hereafter be formed out of unorganized territory of the State must conform to the same rule.

The county organization and form of self-government may be outlined as follows: The county is divided into four precincts, in each of which a commissioner is elected by popular vote every two years. These four commissioners, with the county judge, who is elected every two years by the popular vote of the county, constitute the county or commissioners' court. This court bears the same relation to the county as the Legislature does to the State, and for beneficial local institutions it is by far the wisest and most important body. The county judge presides at the meetings and votes only in cases of a tie. He fills a vacancy of a commissioner's office by appointment from the district left vacant. This court has power to fill any other county office left vacant. This court meets in regular session on the second Monday in February, May, August, and November of each year, and the county judge or any three commissioners may call a special session, which may continue until the business for which it was called is completed. A quorum—three commissioners and the county judge—may transact any business except to levy the county tax, when the full number must be present. To this court all petitions for the establishment of schools, roads, bridges, and other local public institutions must be addressed. The general supervision of all property belonging to the county, such as jails, court-houses, poor-houses and poor-farms, is vested in this body. For the erection and maintenance of any of these necessary county institutions, the commissioners' court may levy and collect a tax upon any property within the county that is taxed by the State. The county tax cannot exceed one-half the State tax on any property, except for the purpose of erecting public buildings, and this right is continually subject to constitutional and legislative limitations. An instance of this exception is in building or completing a court-house, when a tax not exceeding fifty cents on the one hundred dollars' valuation may be levied. On the second Monday in June, the commissioners' court meets as a board of equalization, to receive all the assessment lists and books for inspection, equalization and approval. Here the local grievances of the individual citizen are examined and redressed according to popular justice and law. The commissioners' court of any organized county has the full power of local legislation over any adjacent unorganized territory.

The commissioners' court divides the county into eight precincts, and elects a justice of the peace for each. In cities of eight thousand or more inhabitants two justices of the peace are elected and qualified. This court also has power to elect a County Superintendent of Education when necessary. It is the duty of the superintendent to visit the public schools, lecture to them, advise the teachers, and hold teachers' institutes monthly.

The court may elect a County Superintendent of Roads, or a superintendent for each precinct, and also overseers under each superintendent. The court in every case defines the road districts and apportions the hands under the overseers. The court must make a report of the financial condition of the county at each and every regular session, and this report must be published in some local newspaper or posted in four public places in the county. The county clerk makes and keeps a record of all proceedings of the commissioners' court.

The sheriff executes all legal and legislative processes. He is collector of taxes in counties of less than ten thousand inhabitants. He may appoint deputies, but he is personally responsible for their official acts. In counties of less than eight thousand population, one officer may be elected to fill both offices of district and county clerk. A constable is elected for each justice precinct. He must execute and return all processes handed him by any legal officer. Other county officers, whose duties are sufficiently defined by their titles, are assessor of taxes, collector of taxes (in counties of over ten thousand population), surveyor, animal and hide inspector, county attorney, county jury commissioners, and treasurer.

TOWNS.

A town or village containing two hundred inhabitants or less than one thousand may be incorporated as a town by at least twenty inhabitants of such town or village filing an application for incorporation in the office of the county judge, stating the name and the boundaries of the proposed town or village. If all the requisites of incorporation are fulfilled, the county judge orders an election, in which all qualified voters who reside and have resided within the limits of the proposed town or village for the six months next preceding may participate. A majority of the votes polled is sufficient for incorporation. Within twenty days after the election the county judge makes a record in the commissioners' court of the incorporation. After this entry upon the county records the town or village "is a corporation having power to sue and be sued, plead and be impleaded, and to hold and dispose of real and personal property; provided such real property is situated within the limits of the corporation." The county judge then orders an election of a mayor, a marshal, and five aldermen. The jurisdiction of the mayor in civil and criminal cases is the same as that of a justice of the peace. He is the executive of the town ordinances and by-laws. The council, composed of the mayor and the five aldermen, may make by-laws not inconsistent with the constitution and laws of the State; may levy a tax not exceeding one-fourth of one per cent. on the one hundred dollars valuation. The marshal has the same official functions as a constable and, of course, other duties made necessary from the town ordinances and by-laws. He also assesses and collects the taxes.

Cities of one thousand or more inhabitants may be chartered by general laws. Such charter gives express power to levy, assess and collect an annual tax to defray the current expenses of the city government; but such tax can never exceed for any one year one-fourth of one per cent. Cities may hold and dispose of real and personal property situated within or without the corporate limits. Cities of over ten thousand inhabitants may have their charters granted by special acts of the legislature, and may levy a tax on property taxed by the State within the city limits not exceeding two and one-half per cent. The cities having special charters must in all cases provide a tax sufficient to pay interest on all outstanding debts.

The municipal government of the city consists of a city council composed of the mayor and two aldermen from each ward, a majority of whom constitute a quorum for the transaction of business, except at called meetings for the imposition of taxes, when two-thirds of a full board are required, unless otherwise specified. The other officers of the corporation are a treasurer, assessor and collector, a secretary, a city attorney, a marshal, and a city engineer, and such other officers and agents as the city council may from time to time direct. The above-named officers are elected by the qualified electors of the city, and hold their offices for two years and until the election and qualification of their successors. It is so arranged that one alderman is to be elected from each ward every year. The city usually has its powers defined in its charter, and may generally exercise any needful internal police power within its limits, subject only to the limitations of the State constitution and laws.

SCHOOLS.

In 1829 provision was made for the establishment of a " school of mutual instruction " in the capital of each department of State. The curriculum comprised " reading, writing, arithmetic, the dogma of the Catholic religion, and all of Ackermann's catechisms of arts and sciences." Parents who

were able to pay were charged fourteen and eighteen dollars
per annum, according to the advancement of the pupil. The
teachers were paid monthly fixed salaries, in advance. If the
tuition, legacies and private donations were not a sufficient
available fund, the municipal funds were subject to the delin-
quency. Special but limited arrangements were made for
educating some of the poor children at these schools. The
parents who could afford to educate their children were required to do it, under moderate penalties.

The Congress of Texas, after it became a republic, appropriated seventeen thousand seven hundred and twelve acres
of land to each county for public school purposes, and to each
new county the same amount was to be appropriated. This
law still obtains in Texas. The county commissioners may
rent the lands, adding the rental to the available county school
fund, or they may sell the lands and invest the proceeds in
United States bonds, State or county bonds, or in other secu-
rities subject to restrictions provided by law, and the income
from such investment is added to the available county school
fund. It has recently been recommended by the Superintendent of Public Instruction that the proceeds from the
county school lands be loaned to the county for the erection
of school buildings, each district bonding its debt with reas-
onable interest.

The Perpetual School Fund consists of bonds, land, notes
and cash, as follows:

County bonds: $2,622,620; income, $170,000.
State bonds: $2,048,800; income, $130,000.
Railroad bonds: $1,763,317; income, $80,000.
Land notes: $12,743,000; income, $775,000.
Cash on hand: $500,000.

The total amount of permanent school fund in 1890 was
$19,600,000. The income from this fund is nominally about
$1,157,000, but as much of the interest on the land notes is
unpaid, the actual receipts in 1890 were about $885,000.

The State available school fund comprises this income from
the permanent school fund and one-fourth the revenue from

the State occupation taxes, a poll tax of one dollar on every male inhabitant between twenty and sixty years of age, and an annual State tax not exceeding twenty cents on the one hundred dollars valuation. Then the county available school fund adds about half a million dollars, and local taxation adds another half million dollars.

The State available fund is apportioned annually to the several counties, according to the scholastic population of each, for the maintenance of public free schools. The laws purporting to govern the public free schools of Texas declare that the available funds will be " sufficient to maintain and support the public free schools of this State for a period of not less than six months in each year." The reports of 1889-90 show that in the " district school " counties the average term per annum was only five months, and in the " community " counties only 4.83 months. In the cities the average term was 7.62 months. On the first Monday in October of 1884 all but seventy-five of the two·hundred and forty-five counties were divided into convenient school districts by the county courts, and these districts cannot be changed, except by a majority vote of the legal voters in all districts affected by such change. In each district three trustees are elected by the qualified State voters in such district, and these trustees form a body corporate, that is, they may contract, sue and be sued, plead and be impleaded in any court of the State having proper jurisdiction. Any district may, by a two-thirds majority of the qualified property tax-paying voters of the district, levy a tax not exceeding twenty cents on the one hundred dollars valuation of the taxable property of the district. Towns and cities constituting separate and distinct school districts are not limited to this amount, but are subject to such limitations as the respective municipal councils may prescribe.

There is a simpler and more rudimentary system of public free schools for the thinly settled counties and unorganized territory. This is called the " Community System." Any number of *bona fide* residents in any one of these counties may petition the county judge for their *pro rata* of the available annual school fund of the county. As the teacher's salary is based upon the number of pupils in the district or community, a small community is able to have a school for a few months in each year. If the attendance ever falls below thirty-three and one-third per cent. of the enrollment, the trustees must discontinue the school. The county judge appoints the three " community " trustees, and they have all the ordinary powers vested in the trustees of a regular school district, save that they do not constitute a body corporate, and, hence, have not the powers belonging to such a body. Districts, however, may be formed in any of the community counties by the citizens of any section of the county, but must not exceed four square miles in area.

The State Board of Education is composed of the Governor, who is chairman of the board, the Secretary of State, the Comptroller, and the Superintendent of Public Instruction, who is *ex officio* secretary of the board. This board makes the apportionments to the several counties and to the separate and distinct city and town school organizations.

COUNTY SCHOOL OFFICERS.

The County Commissioners' Court is the tribunal to which all petitions and grievances are referred that do not come within the jurisdiction of the board of trustees, such as petitions for a local tax to be added to the available school fund, or a special tax for the erection of school buildings. The county superintendent is an officer chosen at the discretion of the commissioners' court, and his duty is the general superintendence of all public free schools in the county. This general superintendence devolves upon the county judge when no distinctive officer is elected.

In cities, or in towns that are constituted distinct school organizations, six trustees, if a majority of the legal voters consent, are elected, holding office four years, three being elected every two years. The mayor and county judge are *ex officio* members of the board. If no trustees are elected or provided for, the town or city council or board of aldermen exercise the powers that would have been vested in the trustees. The city school districts may issue bonds for the purpose of erecting school buildings, but the county districts cannot. In the districts or communities the " school fund may be used for erecting, furnishing and repairing school-houses," provided the district or community contribute an amount equal to one-third of the school fund for building, and provided a site be donated.

Villages and towns having two hundred inhabitants or more, may incorporate for school purposes alone, by the consent of a majority of the qualified voters living within the proposed district limits. For such a school organization five trustees are elected. It is a duty of the legislature to make provision for a six months' school term. There is a two-mill local tax allowed under the constitution which, if levied, would maintain good schools in the greater number of districts.

In 1889-90 there were 9,065 public schools taught in the State. Of these, the number of graded schools, not including cities, was 307, and the number of ungraded schools, not including cities, was 8,649, and the number of high schools, not including cities, was 109.

W. M. SANDERSON.

NOTE ON TEXAS.[1]

Twenty-six per cent. of the 2,235,523 inhabitants of Texas in 1890 lived in incorporated towns and cities. Four places contained from 23,000 to 38,067 each. Five had between 10,000 and 14,575, and twenty-four had between 3000 and 8300 each, while 329 other places, some of them incorporated, had an average population of 750.

The total receipts for school purposes in 1889-90 were $3,208,965.16. Of this, $377,147.28, or 11.8 per cent., came from local school taxes. The previous year it was 11.5 per cent. The State superintendent of education makes, in his report

---

[1] By the Editor.

for 1889 and 1890, a strong plea for more local taxation, declaring that "not one-tenth of the area of the State is covered by local school tax," but adds that the area so taxing itself is rapidly growing, and that "the law framed in pursuance of the constitutional amendment of 1883, authorizing local taxation, throws many obstacles in the way of the levy of local taxes...The law, as it stands now on our statute books, is distinctly behind public sentiment in this State and ought to be amended."

VI.

LOCAL GOVERNMENT IN ARKANSAS.

Arkansas has the County System. The counties are divided into townships. Each township elects one constable and one justice of the peace for every two hundred electors, but every township must have at least two justices of the peace. These townships have no direct control over their own local affairs, since there is no town-meeting as in the New England States.

The County Court has the real control of all the local affairs of each township, excepting schools and certain matters under the control of the justices of the peace. Each county court has exclusive and original jurisdiction in all matters relating to roads, appointment of viewers and overseers, also in all matters relating to bridges, ferries, paupers and vagrants; it fixes the place of holding elections, purchases property for and sells property of the county, pays out all money for county purposes, and has full control in all other things that may be necessary to the internal improvement and local concerns of the county. This court, composed of the county judge, with a majority of the justices of the peace, meets annually on the first Monday in July, to levy taxes and make appropriations for county purposes. This court regularly meets four times a year, but the county judge, on giving ten days' notice, may hold special sessions. The people biennially elect a sheriff, who is *ex officio* tax collector, unless the legislature appoints a collector. The people also elect a tax assessor, coroner, treasurer, and surveyor, and in each township a constable.

For roads the county court appoints overseers, who call out to work the roads all men between eighteen and forty-five years of age, for not more than five days a year. When a bridge is to be built, the court appoints three viewers to locate the same and report plans. After the completion of the bridge by a contractor, the same three men, who are paid for the service $1.50 a day, decide whether the bridge is built according to the contract. Where there is a swamp, the county court may allow the building of a turnpike and the charging of such tolls by a private company as the court may direct.

The result of all this is that Arkansas has bad roads, except in dry weather. No real effort is put forth to make the roads good. Their working is a sort of annual farce carried out under the· solemn sanction of the law. Who could expect good roads from work of not more than five days in the year? Who could expect competent men to be willing to go as viewers and reviewers of bridges for the sum of one dollar and fifty cents per day?

The county court provides for the poor and the criminal class, and, on petition of a majority of the taxpayers, can purchase a poor-farm and provide a house of correction.

In 1836 Congress offered the State of Arkansas, just admitted as a State, the 16th section of every township and seventy-two sections of land known as the Saline lands. These three land grants from the Federal government were accepted and form the basis of the free school system.

In 1842 the legislature provided for the sale of the 16th section and for the election of trustees in each township. Schools were to be taught for at least four months in each year, and money was also appropriated to buy text-books. In 1867 the legislature levied a tax of twenty cents on the hundred dollars, and provided for a superintendent of public instruction, and also for a school commissioner in each county to examine applicants and grant licenses to teachers. No license had hitherto been required. The congressional township was made the unit of the school district. Unless a school was taught at least three months, the district forfeited its portion of the school revenue belonging to the county; but schools were not free to all until 1868. At that time the

State Board of Education was established, the school fund was increased, and it was decreed that all districts failing to have a school three months a year would forfeit their share of this fund.

This was the beginning of the era of popular education in Arkansas. The prejudice against free schools gave way, and separate schools were provided for the whites and the blacks.

In 1874 another constitutional convention was held, and the present system dates from that time. The State is divided into school districts, numbering 4,448 in 1892.

In addition to a State levy for schools of two mills on every dollar of valuation and a poll tax of one dollar per capita, each of these districts may levy a tax not exceeding five mills. In 1892 nearly sixty-five per cent. of the districts levied this maximum tax, and over twenty per cent. levied from two and one-half to four and one-half mills, and 590 districts, or 13.3 per cent., levied no tax. When it is remembered that in 1889, according to the United States Department of Education, the average State and local tax levy for schools in New England, New York, Pennsylvania, and New Jersey was only 4.39 mills, the total State and local tax of seven mills in Arkansas in 1892 is very creditable, although it only suffices to keep the country schools open about three months in the year.

Of the entire school revenue of $1,096,269.51 in 1892, the State two-mill tax produced $341,621.38, the district tax $571,923.02, the poll tax $167,419.81, and other sources $15,305.30. These items are equivalent to 6.1 mills on the valuation. The State tax for normal and other schools, viz., the blind and deaf mute schools and the State University, adds over half a mill to this.

In 1876, when the district tax was reported for the first time, it amounted to $88,000. In 1884 this had grown to $346,521.26, and in 1892, as stated above, to $571,923.02.

The Superintendent of Public Instruction calls for a reform of the school district system, and suggests the township school system as a substitute. This idea has been endorsed by a

majority of the county superintendents, but as yet no change
has been made.

A school district must contain at least thirty-five persons
between the ages of six and twenty-one years. If a district
be divided by the county court, in accordance with a petition
from a majority of the citizens, both districts must contain
this number. In towns or cities, when twenty voters petition, an election is held, and the town or city, if it so votes,
may become a single district, with six directors. The school
directors, elected by the qualified voters of the district, hire
the teachers, sign orders on the county treasury, purchase a
site for the school-house and provide for the government
of the school.

The chief development of local government in the State is
the annual school-meeting, which resembles the Massachusetts town-meeting, though the powers are limited to school
affairs. The directors must give notice fifteen days before
the annual school-meeting, in which meeting all the qualified
electors in each school district can talk and vote on questions relating to the school. By vote they decide to levy or
not to levy an extra school tax, not exceeding four mills on
the dollar; whether or not there shall be a school, and how
long it shall be taught; select a site for a school-house where
necessary; decide whether a part of their school money shall
go to build a school-house, when one is needed. At the first
annual school-meeting they elect three directors, who are to
serve one, two and three years respectively, and at each sub-
sequent annual school-meeting they elect one director.

Here is a germ which may one day develop into real local
government. The people may be trained in this annual
school-meeting to take such interest in managing their own
local affairs, that in time each township may wish to control
all its own affairs in a similar manner. However, if the people
are moving in this direction, their progress is, like that of a
sluggish stream, scarcely perceptible.

B. W. DODSON.

NOTE ON ARKANSAS.[1]

There were in 1892 nine cities which taxed themselves sufficiently to keep their schools open eight months, and sixty-one towns which, in a similar manner, kept theirs open nearly six months. A most interesting phase of local government in the South is presented by statements in the report for 1892 of Mr. J. H. Shinn, State Superintendent of Public Instruction. He says that though nine-tenths of the school tax is paid by the whites, it is, in most cases, distributed so as to give equal length of school to both races. " Colored men may be elected directors of schools, and are so elected and control the boards of twenty per cent. of the school districts in the State, this being nearly the whole territory occupied by them...The following voluntary statement given by Jake Woods, a colored man in District No. 2, Pulaski county, is a fair sample of what the superintendent hears on all sides as he moves about over the State: ' We have three directors in No. 2, two negroes and one white man. We have no clashing whatever. There are 38 white children and 549 colored children. We have six schools, each of which is kept open free for six months. The negroes have five of these schools and the whites one. The whites pay about all of the taxes, although our race is beginning to gather some property. The white man selects the white teacher and we select the colored teachers. We pay the white teacher $40 per month, and the same to a colored man who holds a first-grade license. My children are improving, and I am satisfied with the schools.' "

---

[1] By the Editor.

VII.

LOCAL GOVERNMENT IN KENTUCKY.

The history of Kentucky has determined the character of her local government, whether it should be of the County or of the Township. Previous to the year 1776, what is now Kentucky was a part of Fincastle Co., Va. In that year Kentucky Co., embracing the present State of Kentucky, was established, with Harrodsburg as the county seat. There, on Kentucky soil, was reinstituted the Southern County, with its Justices, Sheriff, and Quarter Sessions, having the same powers and practices as in the older part of Virginia. In the year 1781 Kentucky County was divided into three,—Jefferson, Lincoln, and Fayette, separated from each other by the Kentucky and Green rivers. Again the Virginia county-machinery was established in each division, with the addition of an officer in charge of the county militia and having the rank of colonel.[1] The work thus fairly begun was carried on to its legitimate end. Every division of the original counties saw a set of officers established in the new county corresponding in every particular to those in the old ones. More recently there have been some irregularities in the names of some of the officers, and in some few cases in the division of work among them. But in general the development has been very uniform, and the counties of Kentucky of the present, as would be expected, are governed much like those of Virginia.

The character of the government of a State is determined very largely by its constitution. Kentucky has had four constitutions. The first was adopted in 1792, the second in 1799, the third in 1848, and the last in 1891. Under the

---

[1] Doubtless the origin of the Kentucky Colonel.

first and second constitutions, all judges, justices, sheriffs, constables, and clerks of courts were appointed by the Governor. The revision of 1848 was effected to make these officers elective. The new constitution of 1891 was necessary, because that of 1848 provided for slavery. The State is at present in a period of transition. The new constitution is in force, but the General Assembly has not yet so revised the statutes as to conform to the constitution. This discussion describes, in the main, the government as it existed under the constitution of 1848, and mentions the fact when the new constitution provides for a change.

County Organization.

Each county of Kentucky has a Judge of the County Court, a Clerk of the County Court, a Sheriff, a County Attorney, an Assessor, a Surveyor, a Coroner, a Superintendent of Schools, a Clerk of the Circuit Court, and a Jailer.

The County Judge is elected by the qualified voters of the county for a term of four years. He is a very important official. He is a magistrate, and has jurisdiction of both civil and criminal causes. He is required to take and approve the bonds of county officials, appoint guardians and administrators and make settlements with them. He establishes magisterial districts and election precincts, appoints election officers, and presides over the Court of Claims.

The Clerk of the County Court is elected for the same term and in the same manner as the county judge. His duties are clerical: to record the proceedings of the county court, to record all deeds and mortgages, to issue marriage licenses, and to be the custodian of all important documents and books.

The Sheriff is ineligible for a third consecutive term of two years. His duties are those usually devolving upon that time-honored officer, and, in addition, he is State and county tax collector.

The County Attorney is elected for four years and has the usual duties of his office.

The Assessor is elected for a term of four years, and receives as compensation a commission on the amount of property assessed. In addition to returning a list of all taxable property, with a full and fair value affixed, he also returns a list of all horses, mules, cattle, stores, pleasure carriages, watches, pianos, gold and silverware, all legal voters, enrolled militia, and children of school age. Upon failure to accept the office after election, he is fined $500. His work is revised by a board of five Supervisors.

The Coroner is in one respect the highest official in the county. He is the only person who has power to arrest an offending sheriff. He may also execute processes in other criminal, penal and civil cases. When so doing, he is governed by the same laws as apply to the sheriff. His other duties are common to all similar officers.

The County Superintendent is elected for four years and receives a stated salary. He is not eligible for election till he has obtained from the State Board of Examiners a certificate of qualification. It is his duty to have general supervision of the common schools, to lay off, alter or abolish districts, to visit schools, to draw moneys due the county for schools, to pay teachers, to make a settlement with the county judge, and report to the State superintendent. This office is frequently held by young law students who know and care very little about schools. The small salary of $200 to $500 helps to tide them over the starving time in a lawyer's life. Only four counties in the State pay as much as $1,000 per year. Incompetent men keep the schools in bad repute, while the low wages have a tendency to keep competent men out of the work.

All these officers must be at least twenty-four years of age, except the clerks of the county and circuit courts, who must be at least twenty-one.

Vacancies in any of these offices, save the county judge and clerk of the circuit court, are filled by the county judge. A vacancy in the county judgeship is filled by the justices of the peace. A vacancy in the office of circuit court clerk is filled by the judge.

Courts.

The Court of Claims is a county court held by the college of justices, two from each magisterial district, and is presided over by the county judge. It meets once each year, but may be convened oftener by the county judge. Its powers and duties are those usually given a board of county commissioners. The new constitution provides that the General Assembly may abolish this court and delegate its powers to a board of four, including the county judge, who shall be president. The duties of the court are "to fix the county levy, to make appropriations for the benefit of the county, to provide for the maintenance of the paupers, to fix the salaries of certain county officers and make appropriations therefor, and do such other acts as may be lawfully required." Among these other acts is its supervision of the sanitary condition of the county and its power to appoint a county health officer and a county physician and fix the salaries of the same. It is the duty of the county physician to attend all the paupers of the county, both in and out of the county poorhouse.

Taxes levied for county purposes must be levied by county authorities. All taxes must be levied for a stated purpose, and all money so collected must be expended for the purpose for which it was levied. All license fees on franchises, or special or excise tax, though regulated by State law, are under the control of local authorities. The court of claims builds all public buildings and has general charge of them, builds bridges, buys lands and erects buildings for the poor, and appoints overseers, and is in short a general administrative body. It will be seen that this board of justices in Kentucky bears a striking resemblance to the English Quarter Sessions prior to the recent changes,—another evidence of the English origin of American institutions.

To assist in the administration of justice, public schools and public roads, the county is divided into three sets of districts each independent of the other. (1) The Magisterial District is the largest of these divisions. Heretofore there has been very little regularity as to the size and number of these dis-

tricts, but the new constitution provides that there shall not
be fewer than three nor more than eight. The new constitution also provides that the General Assembly shall supervise
the formation of new districts. There will now be more
uniformity of size. The Magisterial District serves the double
purpose of a voting precinct and an area of convenient size for
the election of a justice of the peace. In some cases, however, there are two or more precincts in the same magisterial
district. The boundary of the one never extends beyond that
of the other. In some cases these districts have taken on,
in part, the powers and practices of a township, by levying
taxes to build bridges and by subscribing to the stock of railroads. There is at this writing a discussion in the General
Assembly as to whether the taxing district for school purposes shall be the school district or the county. There is a
probability that this matter may be compromised by making
the magisterial district the taxing district for school purposes.
This would be giving the magisterial district another of the
powers of the Northern township. Doubtless in time it will
take on all or nearly all of them.

There are two justices elected in each district every four
years. Each justice holds a regular court every three months,
and may hold a called court for the trial of certain causes.
He has limited jurisdiction in civil causes, is a conservator of
the peace within his county, and can inflict fines and impris-
onment for penal offenses of a certain character. He can
hold investigating trials, when persons are charged with fel-
onies or high crimes, and require bail. He can bind persons
to keep the peace. He is also a member of the court of
claims.

A constable is elected in each magisterial district every two
years. His duties are those usually devolving upon such an
officer. In case a county should fail to elect a sheriff, the
duties of that officer, save that of tax collector, are performed
by the constable. Many of the counties of the State have at
one time or another voted taxes for the construction of rail-

roads, and in some cases have given bonds, before they got the roads, and have never secured them.   In order to keep from paying the taxes, counties have refused to elect a sheriff, whose duty it is to collect the taxes.   The constable performs his other duties and the taxes are farmed out to the lowest bidder.   There is always an understanding that the tax for the road shall never be asked for.

Vacancies in the office of justice or constable are filled by appointment from the Governor of the State,—another relic of the earliest constitutions, in which provision was made that all court officials should be appointed for life by the Governor.

School Districts.

Dr. E. W. Bemis (Johns Hopkins Historical Studies, Vol. I., No. 5) has shown how in the West the school-house has been the nucleus of civil government, as the church was in New England.   Dr. Bemis also prophesied that this would be true of the South.   The prophecy seems to have been realized, in a measure at least, in Kentucky.   The school-meeting in many places resembles very strikingly the town-meeting of Massachusetts.   It is an assembly in which all the qualified voters, including widows, meet to settle by direct vote who shall be trustee, what amount of tax shall be assessed and for what purposes, who shall be the teacher and what his salary. The selection of a teacher and the levying of a tax for repairs, fuel and incidentals are powers which the board of trustees may exercise without consulting the people.   But in many instances even these are submitted to a vote of the people.   I have already shown how this power of levying taxes for school purposes may ere long be given over to the magisterial district, at least the power to levy a tax for teachers' salaries. There is one advantage to be gained by this.   The large and wealthy districts would help to pay the expenses of the small and poor ones.   As it is at present, the small and poor districts must either have a shorter term or pay a higher rate of tax.

School districts are established by the County Superintendent of Schools. No district can include more than one
hundred children of school age, unless it contains a town or a
village within its limits. Each district is under the control of
a board of trustees, three in number, elected by the district.
One must be elected each year for a term of three years to fill
the vacancy made by the one retiring. The chairman is the
one having the shortest time to serve. The board is a body
politic. They may rent or buy property for school purposes.
They may levy a tax to repair a school-house, to supply fuel,
etc. Until recently the board could levy no tax without a
vote of the people. It was hard to get the voters to vote a
tax, until it was absolutely necessary. As a result of the new
law a great improvement in school property is noticed. The
trustees have general control of the schools. They can
employ teachers, and may remove them for cause, subject to
the approval of the county superintendent. They must take
the school census and report the same to the superintendent
along with other matters showing the general condition of the
school. For neglect of duty they are subject to fine and
removal. As a matter of fact there are very few who do not
sorely neglect their duties.

The school fund is derived from several sources. The
State levies a direct tax of 22 cents on $100 worth of tax-
able property. There is a sinking fund of about $3,000,000,
on which the State pays 6 per cent. interest. Certain counties
hold State bonds, the interest on which goes into the school
fund. All this the State distributes to the several districts,
in proportion to the number of children of school age. This
can be used only to pay salaries. Many districts supplement
this by a tax or voluntary subscription to prolong the school.
Many rural districts have received permission from the State
by special act of legislature to form themselves into corporations, with special rights and privileges, to establish a system
of school with high school department. These seem to work
well, but always meet with more or less opposition from the
large property-holders who have no children to send to school.

I give below such selected statistics as may be helpful in forming an idea of the working of the Kentucky schools.

ITEMS.	WHITE.		COLORED.	
	1888.	1891.	1888.	1891.
Number of districts........	6,628	6,815	1,004	1,060
Number of schools taught				
five months..............	5,329	5,529	774	785
four months..............	733	741	94	120
three months.............	556	530	118	147
School census..............	549,732	573.704	107,170	112,815
Enrolled in schools........	344.856	360.913	51,180	55,474
Per cent of attendance.....	35	37	26	28
Tuition per month:				
county schools,......	76c	83c	92c	1.02
city com. "	$1.17	$1.18	88c	98c
city high "	$2.84	$3.33	$2.50	$1.90
Average wages per month,				
male and female.........	31.21	34.62	34.87	41.51
Average wages city com-				
mon schools, males......	131.51	128.22	59.51	60.55
females	48.31	48.27	42.69	43.93
Average wages city high				
schools, males...........	134.28	151.00	95.00	83.30
females.........	79.34	78.97	....	....
School money, State app'mt.	104,448	1,290.834	203,623	253,840
" local tax.....	558.835	716,166	22,648	23,015
Per capita, State...........	1.90	2.25	1.90	2.25
" local tax	1.01	1.23	.21	.20
" int. county bonds	.04	.04	.04	.04
Av. school term, country...	5 mos.	5 mos.	5 mos.	5 mos.
" " city.......	9 mos.	9 mos.	9 mos.	9 mos.

ROAD DISTRICTS.

Some counties keep their roads in repair by a direct property tax. The roads are then let out to the lowest bidder. It is the business of this person to keep the roads in order; he lays himself liable to a fine if he fails to do so. Under this system one man is made responsible for the condition of the roads, and the people see, generally, that he does his duty. The system works well, and the writer does not know of a single instance where a county has gone back to the old plan after trying this. Under the old system, and that generally in use, the county judge divides the county into a number of districts of convenient size, and appoints a surveyor for each district. It is the duty of this surveyor to notify "all male persons over sixteen and under fifty years of age" to appear at such time and place as he may direct, to work the roads. In this way the roads are kept in order by a sort of poll-tax.

MUNICIPALITIES.

The entire population of Kentucky, according to the census of 1890, is 1,858,635. The then population in incorporated towns and cities was 503,216, or 27 per cent. of the entire census. The per centum of urban population is greatly on the increase. In some cases the rural districts have lost, while the cities and towns universally show a decided increase. Again, owing to the building of railroads and the growth of towns about the stations, the number of the towns is constantly and rapidly increasing. In 1880 eleven cities had a population each of more than 4000. In 1890 the number of that size was sixteen. The aggregate population of the eleven in 1880 was 231,720; that of the sixteen in 1890 was 325,289,—an increase in the population of cities of this size of 93,569, or 40.38 per cent., while Winchester, Henderson, Richmond, Paducah, Owensboro, and Bowling Green each showed an increase of more than 50 per cent.

The urban districts of Kentucky are divided into three classes by their forms of government. A city is a municipality, having complete self-government by means of a mayor and a council. A town is an incorporated district wanting some of the forms and many of the privileges of a city. A village is an unincorporated town. There are at present in Kentucky twenty-five cities, two hundred and forty-eight towns, and more than one thousand villages. The government of the cities and towns is based upon special charters granted by the General Assembly. There is such a want of uniformity in their government as to make description very difficult. Happily, a description is not necessary. The new constitution provides for complete uniformity in the future.

Section 163 of the new constitution says: "The cities and towns of this commonwealth, for the purposes of their organization and government, shall be divided into six classes. The organization and powers of each class shall be provided for by the general laws so that all municipal corporations of the same class shall possess the same powers and be subject to the same restrictions. To the first class shall belong cities with a population of one hundred thousand or more, and the city of Louisville is hereby declared a city of first class; to the second class, cities with a population of thirty thousand or more and less than one hundred thousand; to the third class, cities with a population of eight thousand or more and less than thirty thousand; to the fourth class, cities and towns with a population of three thousand or more and less than eight thousand; to the fifth class, cities and towns with a population of one thousand or more and less than three thousand; to the sixth class, towns with a population of one thousand or less." According to this provision the classification will be as follows:

CLASS.	NUMBER.	AGGREGATE POP.	AVERAGE POP.
1	1	161,129	161,129
2	1	37,371	37,371
3	5	79,954	15,591
4	16	71,444	4,561
5	39	62,518	1,609
6	216	90,800	425

Besides these there are some fifteen hundred villages of various sizes. About one thousand of these have an average population of one hundred. Some of these have a population of one thousand or more, and many of them more than five hundred. A large number of these will doubtless be organized as towns under the new constitution.

The new constitution fixes a maximum rate of taxation in the municipalities of the different classes. It also fixes the amount of bonds which any taxing district may issue, at a certain per cent. of the taxable property, differing in the different classes. The new constitution likewise fixes a maximum limit of the time for which bonds and franchises may be given. It provides for certain reforms in city government by requiring that many of the councilmen and members of the school board shall be elected by the city at large, and by prohibiting all bills of a local nature, which have been the curse of good government in Kentucky. All local government must now be provided for by general laws.

The outlook for improvement in the local institutions in Kentucky is very bright. In no time in the history of the State have the people taken so great a part in the management of local affairs. The people are beginning to understand that the nearer a home government is to a people the better it is likely to be and the less the liability of fraud. The writer predicts that Kentucky will ere long take on a form of local administration resembling that of Illinois or Indiana.

J. W. FERTIG.

VIII.

MISSOURI.

It has been often pointed out that the fatal weakness of the French as colonizers consisted in the fact that local government had no place in their colonial system. There was no individual initiative among them, so that, when they came into competition with the American pioneers of the Northwest, they were soon completely distanced in their attempts at settlement. When the United States acquired the territory of Louisiana, several quite important settlements already existed within the present limits of the State of Missouri. Of the total population of these settlements, 3,760 were French, together with a few Spaniards, 5,000 Anglo-Americans, and 1,300 blacks, for the most part slaves. French customs prevailed. Trade had been retained in the hands of a close corporation, and the entire control of affairs had been highly paternal. Yet the people had prospered fairly well, for both France and Spain had sent them good and wise.governors. Progress was, however, very slow, and the outlook for any considerable increase of settlement most unpromising.

Soon after the United States came into possession of Louisiana, Congress passed an act dividing it into two parts, the Territory of Orleans (now the State of Louisiana) and the District of Louisiana. As by far the greater part of the French people resided in the Territory of Orleans, this division allowed the Americanizing tendencies of the District of Louisiana to assert themselves more quickly and effectually. The same act which divided the territory also made the District of Louisiana, or " Upper Louisiana," a part of the executive department of Indiana under Gen. W. H. Harrison. Under the supervision of Gov. Harrison much of what is now the State of Missouri was divided into four districts, each having a civil and a military commandant.

On the 3d of March, 1805, the District of Louisiana was regularly organized into the Territory of Louisiana, and President Jefferson appointed Gen. Wilkinson governor of the new territory. Gov. Wilkinson, together with the three judges of the Superior Court, made up a legislative board for the territory, the first distinct step toward its local government.

In 1812 the Territory of Missouri was organized, and on the 1st of October of the same year Governor Clark issued a proclamation as required by Congress, reorganizing the four quasi-military districts, formed by Gen. Harrison, into five counties. Since that time the county has remained the almost exclusive civil division for local purposes in the State. Within the last two decades, however, the township, having won a permanent place in the Northwest, has been making its way slowly to the southward, as the old conditions resulting from slavery have yielded slowly to the new order of industrial growth, with its more sharply marked local interests.

As the early settlers of Missouri were, for the most part, from Kentucky, Virginia, and other Southern States, it was but natural that the county should be adopted as the chief and only local division. All of Illinois and large parts of Kentucky and Tennessee were at times counties of Virginia and North Carolina. In the settlement of the West the county has always preceded the township. This is chiefly because of its judicial functions. It is more easily adopted, as it is more artificial and built less upon special local habits and customs than is the township. It secures law and order, the first great necessities of frontier communities. Some new town centrally located is usually selected as a county seat, where all county records may be safely kept, those of land entries being of the most immediate and vital importance to a new and rapidly increasing settlement. The services of the county surveyor, an officer with little to do in an older community, are in constant demand, thus emphasizing the importance of the county.   For a while, people content themselves with very poor roads, frequently going long distances to avoid sloughs or to find fordable crossings over large streams.   Such few large bridges as are indispensable the county can best construct, so, in any case, there is little necessity for township road management.   Paupers are of the rarest occurrence in such communities.   Every one is self-reliant.   What each most desires is to be assured of a safe title to his land and protection against the outlaws which so often infest frontier settlements.   But even this evil he sometimes overcomes by forming with his scattered neighbors a vigilance committee, which strikes evil-doers with terror.   In no part of the country have these various phases of frontier life been better exhibited than in the States of the Southwest, where the Virginia county has been uniformly adopted.

When Missouri became a State in 1821, the five original counties had been subdivided into twenty, and the first State legislature passed a general law for county organization.   All county business was vested in a court to consist of three judges styled " justices of the county court."   This court was to have original jurisdiction over all matters of county concern, to appoint guardians, fix county lines, conduct elections, raise revenue, build bridges and regulate taverns.   The court was authorized to divide the county into three districts, each one of which was to elect a county judge.   The county has been changed many times since its adoption, though not materially save once.   Most of the changes prior to the civil war were toward a greater centralization of power in the court. The one notable exception to the continued organization of the court, as thus outlined, occurred in 1825, and is chiefly of interest as a freak of American legislation.   Its purpose, obviously, was to remove the control of local affairs as far as possible from the people, and it was an invention of State interference in local matters not unworthy of comparison with some of the best efforts of French statesmanship.   A law was passed making the court to consist for one year of all the justices in the county.   At the close of the first year this tem-

porary court was to select not less than three nor more than
seven justices to constitute a court for the following year, and
in this way the members of the court were to appoint their
successors at the end of each year. The justices were not
elected by the people, but, after a cumbrous process of nomi-
nation, were selected by State authority. Upon petition of
twenty white citizens it became the duty of the county court
to make out a list of persons suitable as justices of the peace.
Out of this list the State senator or representative from that
county or district nominated certain ones, who were elected
by the legislature and approved by the Governor. Thus, inter-
mediate between the people and the county court, stood the
State government, while the court itself was self-perpetuating.
This system very soon broke down from its own weight, and
the court was again made to consist of three judges as before.

As constituted at present, the county court consists of three
judges, two of whom are elected for two years. For this purpose the county is divided as nearly as may be into two equal
districts, each of which elects a judge. The third judge is
elected by the county at large for four years and is president
of the court. The court has lost most of its judicial powers.
In a few cases, not otherwise provided for by law, it still has a
right to summon witnesses and to examine them on oath
touching any matter in controversy. While the court has a
considerable range of legislative privileges prescribed by
statute, its chief functions now are of an administrative character. It exercises control over all property, real and personal, belonging to the county, and has a wide latitude of discretionary powers to devise ways and means for the same. It
is also the duty of the court to audit, adjust and settle all
accounts to which the county is a party; to order the payment,
out of the county treasury, of any sum of money found due by
the county on such account, and to order suit to be brought
by the prosecuting attorney, in the name of the county, against
any delinquent. It has control of the county finances, directs
the levy of taxes, and sits with the county clerk, surveyor, and
assessor as a board of equalization to adjust the assessment of
property for taxation. It is also custodian and manager of

the school funds of the county, and exercises supervision over all county officers. It is in fact the superintendent of all county interests. The law provides that four terms of the court must be held each year. In counties of 75,000 inhabitants it is required to hold a meeting every month. Each judge receives mileage fees and a *per diem* consideration for all time spent in official business.

From the very fact that the county is best suited to the broad, crude conditions of pioneer communities, we may justly infer that, as population becomes denser, local government, to be effective and democratic, should be more localized. Thus only may each citizen have an opportunity to exercise that privilege and responsibility which, under right conditions, should bring out the highest results of citizenship. Very early in the settlement of the Northwest the people from New England began to adopt the township, making it a part of the county and transferring to it the management of all the more strictly local affairs. This went on successfully and naturally in States like Michigan, Wisconsin, and Minnesota, where New Englanders predominated; but in Illinois the first settlers were mostly from Kentucky and Virginia, and the county was of course the ultimate division for local purposes. As the people from New England began at last to pour into Illinois, chiefly into the northern and central parts, a struggle inevitably arose as to whether the county or township should be the chief local unit. ' The new constitution of 1847 compromised the matter by authorizing the legislature to pass a law permitting the people of any county to adopt township organization or not, just as a majority might elect. Under this law many counties voted to adopt the township at once, and others have continued to do so, until only 18 out of 102 counties of Illinois are still without township organization. Not more than two or three counties have ever abandoned the system after having once adopted it.'

---

[1] Letter from Secretary of State Pearson, who also says that the best and perhaps the only argument in favor of county, as compared with township government, is the greater expense of the latter.

Nor has the triumph of the township been due entirely to the fact that New England people came to predominate, for many of the counties which were chiefly settled by Southern people have adopted the system after becoming familiar with its merits. It would thus appear that in Illinois the township has, by a fair test, established its superiority over the county, for purely local purposes. The conditions of Illinois which have exerted a formative influence on its local system approach much nearer to those which produced the township in New England than to those which produced the county in Virginia.

Following the example of Illinois, Missouri inserted a clause into her new constitution of 1875 authorizing the legislature to pass an act making township organization optional with the counties. Previous to this, in 1872, a law was made providing for township organization, but was defective, for several counties, after having tried it, abandoned the system, and the law was repealed. This act provided for too radical a change, for it abolished the county court without providing an efficient substitute. Experience seems to prove that a careful integration of the township and county is required to give the best results. In 1879 an act was passed in accordance with the constitutional provision, and under this law 16 of the 114 counties of the State have adopted township organization.

As organized, the township is a body corporate, with powers to sue and to be sued, to purchase and hold real estate within its own limits for the use of its inhabitants, to make contracts, purchase and hold personal property, and to make all necessary regulations for the use of its corporate property. The functions of the township are all prescribed by statute. At the usual place of voting in each township, biennial meetings of all qualified voters are held for the election of township officers and for the transaction of such other business as may be necessary. The officers to be chosen at these meetings are a trustee, who is also *ex officio* treasurer of the township, a collector, a clerk, a constable, two members of the township board of directors, two justices of the peace, and as many road overseers as there are road districts in the township. The·overseer of any district, however, must be elected by the voters of his own district. Though the law provides that these meetings, besides electing the township officers, shall " transact such other township business as may be necessary," yet these meetings do not, like the New England town-meetings, transact all the township business, but merely vote on certain important measures which it is deemed prudent not to leave entirely to the township officers. The township is represented in its corporate capacity by a board of directors, consisting of two members elected solely as directors, together with one of the township trustees. This board audits all accounts and signs all orders and official acts, including provision for roads and the building of bridges which cost less than $100. It also fills all vacancies in township offices and receives resignations. The board is required by law to meet three times each year and as much oftener as the interests of the township may require. At its first annual meeting the board elects one of its members president, and it is his duty to sign all orders and official acts of the board. The duties of the other township officers are so clearly indicated by their titles that a description of them here is unnecessary. Each officer receives a *per diem* compensation for his services, in addition to which the clerk and treasurer receive special fees.

The smallest corporate body for public purposes in Missouri is the school district. It must contain at least twenty pupils of school age, and must maintain separate schools for white and colored pupils at least six months annually. On the first Tuesday of April the qualified voters of the district, in annual meeting, determine the length of the school term over six months; fix the amount of school levy in excess of 40 cents on $100; vote funds for the school library; decide as to the disposition of school property, location of school-house, and as to changes of boundaries of the district; and ballot for county commissioner or superintendent, and for one of three

school directors, who hold office for three years. The directors elect a president and a clerk and exercise control over the
school property of the district. They make rules for the
organization and grading of the schools, employ teachers,
visit the schools, enumerate the pupils, and estimate to the
county clerk the probable annual cost of maintaining the
schools of the district.

In the formation of school districts little attention has been
paid to county, township or section lines. Frequently a
school district lies in two counties, in two congressional townships and in two municipal townships. " These irregularities
result from several causes. Sometimes streams are impas-
sable or are dangerous to cross, and the boundary line of the
district is made to conform to the course of the stream.
Sometimes the taxable value of the property of a district is
small, and to relieve the burden of taxation a small portion of
another district is added, it may be only a ten-acre tract out
of a man's farm. Small tracts are thus frequently added when
they include a residence and outbuildings. Sometimes a
farm is of irregular outline and extended into a different district from that in which the owner's residence is situated, and
he has the district lines so adjusted as to include all his property in one district. He thus avoids paying taxes in two districts and at different rates. Sometimes neighborhood quar-
rels, petty jealousies and contrariness render it unpleasant for
men to be associated, and they separate by changing the
boundaries of districts."[1]

It is precisely this overlapping of local territorial divisions
which constitutes one of the most serious barriers to the development of the township in Missouri. This fact will be more
easily appreciated after a brief examination of the growth of
the township in other Western States. In the prairie States
of the Northwest, congressional townships, those six-mile
squares into which all land is divided by the United States
survey, have furnished most convenient and natural terri-

---

[1] R. D. Shannon in "Civil System of Missouri."

torial divisions for local corporate purposes, and have been
extensively organized into civil townships. Since the 16th
section of each congressional township is set apart by law for
school purposes, it would seem but natural that the school
district to which the funds arising from this section are to be
devoted should be made to coincide with the township. This
has been the line of development in most of the Western
States, and in some of them laws have recently been enacted
creating each civil township into a school district. It has
therefore been said that the school is the nucleus of the township in the Western States, as the church was in the early
days of New England. Such a course of development, it will
be readily seen, would be greatly hindered, if not prevented,
by the utter lack of coincidence among the local divisions of
Missouri. There is a growing tendency, however, to divide
the school districts so that they will not be in more than one
county or township. A recent statute of Missouri provides
that hereafter, except in certain rare cases, no school district
shall be formed that is divided by a county line.

While the independent school district is more local than the
township school district, it is, as a rule, less efficient. There
are, in nearly all communities, people who are too ignorant or
too indifferent to attend school meetings, or who, when they
do attend, oppose any levy whatever for school purposes. In
the independent districts of some of the Western States a
majority of foreign voters has in this way actually prevented
the erection of school-houses imperatively needed. Such diffi-
culties are largely prevented, and a much more intelligent and
uniform management of the schools is secured, where the
township school district prevails. Such districts are divided
into a number of sub-districts, usually nine, where the township is regular, or six miles square. Each sub-district elects
a director, who, together with the other sub-directors of the
township, constitute a board for the management of the
school affairs of the township. The sub-district, as a rule,
chooses one of its ablest and most public-spirited citizens as
director, and a township board is thus made up of men much

more capable of controlling the township schools wisely than
are the districts themselves. No district can therefore, by a
majority of indifferent or hostile voters, cripple the efficiency
of its school by refusing it necessary funds. Owing to the
superiority of the township school district it has been rapidly
coming into favor in most of the Northern States, and is fav-
ored by most superintendents of public education both North
and South. Missouri is no exception to the rule.

One of the objections urged against the township system
in Missouri, and indeed the chief objection, is that it is more
expensive than the county system. If, however, the township
system were made to control the public school as well as other
local functions, it is not improbable that enough would be
saved in this one item to pay all the running expense of the
township. There is no reason why this would not hold good
in Missouri as well as in the older States of the North. The
more nearly all the different local interests of the community,
whether pertaining to the school, the roads, or taxation, are
identified with the township, the more efficiently will they be
administered and the more strongly will the township com-
mand the respect and attachment of the people.

While but comparatively few of the counties of Missouri
have township organization, the movement of all legislation
on local matters, in the last few years, has been toward township development. From the earliest pioneer days the county
has been divided into districts, known as municipal townships, which, contrary to what their name would indicate,
have no municipal privileges. In use they correspond
closely to the precinct of the early Virginia county, as they
existed merely for county purposes. As the counties have
been reduced in size, these municipal townships have been
made smaller by the county court, so that their present size
has suggested a convenient enlargement of local administration. This occurred in 1888, when the legislature passed an
act incorporating the municipal township for road purposes.
Each municipal township in the State, except those having the
regular township organization, was declared to be a body

corporate for road purposes only, by the name of "—— road township." These townships were given entire control of road matters, such as belonged to the organized townships, including the power to levy taxes not exceeding in any one year 40 cents on the $100 of assessed valuation of all taxable property in the township.

In counties having township organization the people seem for the most part to be very much attached to it. It relieves those who live in distant parts of the county from the necessity of going to the county-seat on purpose to pay their taxes. The people of the township are much more interested in the improvement of the roads than is the county court, and larger levies are more readily obtained. As a matter of fact the highest levies for road purposes are said to be in the organized townships, a fact which should be borne in mind, when the expense of the township is compared unfavorably with that of the county, for such an expense is indeed an investment yielding an increased return. The county court is often indifferent to the needs of a particular part of the county, and dispenses its official favors so as to requite political support. Indeed, it is quite frequently charged with corruption, and there is much to give color to such charges. Under township organization it is claimed that the collection of taxes is much closer than otherwise, thus making up in part for the increased expense of the township. There are some who oppose the township system because of the great number of local officers necessary under it. These officers, they claim, are too ignorant, as a rule, to perform efficiently the duties required of them. This objection was made to the writer by several county judges. It is generally conceded, however, that while there is some ground for this charge at first, yet, after a time, it disappears, showing conclusively that the township is a great educator in local government, which is indeed one of the highest claims urged in its favor by all writers from De Tocqueville to Bryce.

Of the sixteen counties having township organization, twelve are in the northwest part of the State and four are in the western tier south of the Missouri river. The last census report shows that there are in all of these counties more people of Northern than of Southern nativity, a fact which largely explains the adoption of the township in these counties. The foreign population is very light, which should be favorable to good local government. Nor is this advantage counterbalanced by the negro population, for in ten of the counties these people do not make up four per cent. of the population, while in the other six they form less than ten per cent.; nor are the proportions greatly different in a large part of the State. But one county has ever abandoned the township system as provided for by the act of 1879, and that was done merely to escape a special tax unwisely, if not unjustly, voted upon some of the townships. There is already a movement on foot, however, to reorganize the townships.[1] This is a significant fact, which the opponents of the township system, and especially the State officials, do not notice, for they give great weight to the fact that several counties have abandoned township organization, making no distinction whatever between counties organized according to the defective act of 1872 and those as organized at present in accordance with the act of 1879. For a great part of Missouri, however, the county is undoubtedly the best form of local government. The people are familiar with no other form, and population will not be dense for a long time to come. It is equally plain, however, that there are many other counties in which the present county system is becoming more unsatisfactory and that it must give way to a system in which the people shall have a greater share of activity. There are doubtless many defects in the present township system which will need to be remedied by the legislature. It can, indeed, scarcely be doubted that a concentration in the township of all the more strictly local functions would result in a system much more

---

[1] The statements in the last few lines are derived from Prof. J. T. Ridgway, who is preparing a careful treatise on the working of local government in Missouri, and who has kindly given me several items of interest on the subject.

economical and effective than exists at present. Nor has the
township had time as yet to adjust itself to the county system,
and it is equally evident that the county organization will
need to be modified so as to admit of a more perfect adjust-
ment between its functions and those of the townships.
Meanwhile there is growing up a political self-consciousness
in regard to local affairs on the part of the people which
promises much for reforms in this line.

There are also some purely political reasons urged as of
decisive importance as to whether the county or township
shall prevail. The presiding judge of a county court ended
a list of charges against the township by saying that "finally
he was opposed to township organization because his party,
which had a good majority in the county, could not elect its
ticket in some of the townships." This, however, should
incline the people to favor the township rather than to oppose
it, for their interests are not foremost with the spoilsman who
would bestow all local offices as a reward for party service.
There is much less partisanship in township than in county
elections, and men are chosen with reference to their qualifications and efficiency more than to their party allegiance.

The cities and villages of Missouri, except St. Louis, re-
main parts of the counties in which they are situated. They
are incorporated by act of the county court, and their rights
and privileges are determined by statute. St. Louis receives
special mention in the constitution, and its relation to the State
is the same as that of a county. Cities are divided into four
classes, 500 inhabitants being the lowest limit of a city of the
fourth or lowest class. All towns containing less than 500
people are known as villages, which may or may not be incorporated. If unincorporated, the village is governed by the
township or county in which it is situated. Upon application
of two-thirds of its taxable citizens a village may be incorporated by the county court, when its incorporation becomes
similar to that of a city. In cities of the fourth class the legislative department is known as the "Board of Aldermen"; in
cities of the third class, which must contain at least four
wards, as the "Council"; in cities of the second class, as the

" Common Council," made up of two councilmen from each
ward; and in cities of the first class as the " Municipal Assembly," which consists of a council of thirteen members
elected by the city at large, and a House of Delegates, composed of a member from each ward in the city, all elected for
four years. In cities of the fourth class the mayor appoints
the Treasurer, Collector, Street Commissioner, and City Attorney. In cities of the third class he appoints the Street
Commissioner and such other officers as he may be authorized
by ordinance to appoint. The Clerk, Engineer, Assessor,
Counselor, and Comptroller are appointed by the mayor in
cities of the second class. In cities of the first class the Attorney, Jailer, Assessors, and the Superintendents and Commissioners of the various public works are appointed by the
mayor in concurrence with the council. The charter of St.
Louis, adopted August 22, 1876, contains some safeguards
against municipal abuse which are worthy of attention, as
they have proved to work most satisfactorily, although there,
as elsewhere, it has been proved that no machinery, however
perfect, will atone for failure to elect competent rulers. One
of the most important of these safeguards at St. Louis is that
which provides that the chief offices to be filled by the
mayor's appointment shall not become vacant until the beginning of the third year of his term of office. Owing to this
provision, appointments by the mayor as rewards for political
support suffer a serious inconvenience and have much less
influence upon elections than formerly.[1]

Such, in brief, is an outline up to the present time of local
government in Missouri, together with some of the influences
which are now making for its more complete development in
the future. It seems more than probable that the township
which, under one name or another, has come down as one of
the most valuable inheritances of the English race, will become the ultimate basis of local government in Missouri.

J. E. NORTHUP.

---

[1] See " The City Government of St. Louis," by Prof. Snow, in
Johns Hopkins University Studies for April, 1887.

NOTE ON MISSOURI.[1]

Of the $5,266,564.09 received in 1891-2 for teachers' salaries and incidentals, aside from school buildings, sixty per cent. was raised by local district taxation, and most of the remainder came from the proceeds of government land grants.

---

[1] By the Editor.

www.ingramcontent.com/pod-product-compliance
Lightning Source LLC
Chambersburg PA
CBHW032245080426
42735CB00008B/1009